GILL'S STUDIES IN IRISH LITERATURE
Terence Brown, General Editor

JOHN BANVILLE
A Critical Study

The essence of Romanticism... comes to consist in that which cannot be described.
　　　　　　　　　　　Mario Praz, *The Romantic Agony*

For, to me there seems to be a manifest Dilemma in the Case: If you explain them, they are Mysteries no longer; if you fail, you have laboured to no purpose.
　　　　　　　Jonathan Swift, *A Letter to a Young Gentleman*

GILL'S STUDIES IN IRISH LITERATURE

JOHN BANVILLE

A Critical Study

JOSEPH McMINN

GILL AND MACMILLAN

Published in Ireland by
Gill and Macmillan Ltd
Goldenbridge
Dublin 8
with associated companies in
Auckland, Delhi, Gaborone, Hamburg, Harare,
Hong Kong, Johannesburg, Kuala Lumpur, Lagos, London,
Manzini, Melbourne, Mexico City, Nairobi,
New York, Singapore, Tokyo
© Joseph McMinn 1991
Print origination by Irish Typesetters
Printed in England by Billing & Sons Ltd, Worcester
All rights reserved. No part of this publication may be copied,
reproduced or transmitted in any form or by any means,
without permission of the publishers.

British Library Cataloguing in Publication Data
McMinn, Joseph
  John Banville: a critical study.
  1. Fiction in English. Banville, John, 1945–
  I. Title
  823.914

ISBN 0-7171-1803-7

*For
Edna*

Contents

Preface	ix
Introduction	1
1. Long Lankin	13
2. Nightspawn	21
3. Birchwood	30
4. Doctor Copernicus	46
5. Kepler	68
6. The Newton Letter	88
7. Mefisto	98
8. The Book of Evidence	109
9. Conclusion	124
Notes	126
Select Bibliography	135
Index	137

Preface

ANYONE with a serious interest in John Banville's fiction, and the literary reputation it has rightly achieved, will acknowledge the pioneering contribution of Rüdiger Imhof. In writing my own study of Banville, I am only too aware of the importance and value of that contribution, beginning with the *Irish University Review* Special Issue on Banville, which appeared nearly ten years ago, continuing with a variety of essays and articles which led to his book-length study. While I warmly acknowledge my debt to this original and systematic work, which emphasises the formalist element in Banville above all else, my own approach, which concentrates on the poetic character of the fiction, offers a very different and, I hope, complementary perspective.

As far as the modern Irish novel is concerned, however, I do not accept Rüdiger Imhof's way of recommending Banville's experimental fiction through a dismissal of the realistic tradition. To characterise, as he does, most twentieth-century Irish novelists and their critics as hopelessly provincial, too narrowly concerned with what he calls 'cosy realism', is to deny talent and significance to all others, and to argue, rather unreasonably, that the best Irish fiction is never about Ireland. The relationship between the realistic and the non-realistic novel is not, I believe, a hierarchical one: neither is 'provincial' an innocent or objective term in comparative literary study. Would Günter Grass be less provincial if he wrote about Ireland instead of Germany?

I would like to thank Terence Brown for suggesting and inviting the present study, and Jonathan Williams for continued and generous help in its completion. I must also thank my friend and colleague, Bill Lazenbatt, for giving a draft-version of the study his close and constructive attention, and for making many valuable suggestions. Above all, I thank my wife for her patient and perceptive help throughout the preparation of this study. She remains, as always, the better critic.

Belfast, 1990

Introduction

THE present study aims to provide a reading of Banville's work which emphasises the imaginative strategies and patterns of that ambitious fiction, and to suggest its place in the context of modern literature. Although he had been writing for twenty years and was highly respected as a serious novelist, it was not until *The Book of Evidence* that Banville's achievement was recognised by a much wider audience. In 1989, that novel was shortlisted for the Booker Prize, and then won the Guinness Peat Aviation Award, Europe's biggest literary prize, designed 'to identify and celebrate the best in contemporary Irish writing'. This success naturally awakened interest in Banville's earlier work, a series of highly imaginative fictions in the tradition of the self-conscious, experimental novel. This more inclusive perspective shows, as it does in the work of many great novelists, a keen sense of artistic purpose and formal progression. The most illuminating context for understanding Banville's work is the one he has crafted and designed out of literature itself.

With a writer like Banville, so receptive to the rhythms of European literature, and so able to select the most suitable literary company for the purposes of his own aesthetic, we would do well to recall some of the major trends of modern literary culture. The innovator in Banville turns out to be a deceptive traditionalist. His fiction, at once tragic and playful, is largely about the recreation of fictions. In this sense, we are faced with a writer who keeps returning to literature itself, a history of the imaginative life, for inspiration.

Banville makes us work for our pleasure. A writer who is so sensitive to the work of other writers keeps us on our toes, but we should remember always that the point of such a deeply referential fiction is to enrich the imaginative range of the work, and thereby the response of the reader, rather than play a scholarly game. This fiction is rich with ideas about illusion and perception, yet the irony of any uncritical fascination with the purely intellectual dimension of the writing is that it may very likely lose sight of the humanistic ideal at the heart of Banville's fiction. The pattern of discovery in, for example, the novels about the great astronomers, Copernicus, Kepler and Newton, could offer us a way of reading Banville. Each of these figures comes to learn something simple, even obvious, but only after great effort and commitment. They *earn* their enlightenment. Banville is essentially a poetic novelist,[1] whose ultimate meaning rests with image and metaphor; but that kind of meaning, if it is to be experienced imaginatively and persuasively, must be dramatised through a testing and difficult fiction. Faced with confusion and isolation, Banville's narrators find small, but precious, consolation in the fictions of Beauty. Their voices belong to modern literature's sense of outrage and shock at the irrationality of the world.

Writing in 1920, the Hungarian critic, Georg Lukács, considered the modern novel as 'the epic of a world that has been abandoned by God'.[2] This proposition gives us a most appropriate starting-point for considering the historical context of Banville's kind of fiction. Contrasting the epic literature of classical civilisation with that of contemporary Europe, Lukács argued that modern literature was characterised by what he called a 'transcendental homelessness' which reflected the breakdown of traditional cultural and political unities. Modernism, as exemplified in Joyce's *Ulysses* (1922), may be seen as an attempt to create an alternative epic, one that celebrates and elaborates that fallen world, the world of the everyday and the commonplace. Every modernist novel has to define itself in relation to Joyce's mock-epic, a narrative that draws its mythic strength as much from daily phenomena as from the classical world. Modernist fiction creates a self-sufficient world, in which the artist replaces God. It is inventive, playful, learned, iconoclastic and outwardly apolitical. Unlike realistic fiction, against which it always measures its own freedom and daring, it makes a literary virtue of subjectivism and alienation, giving full expression to the wealth of the imaginative and fantastical mind of its narrators. The voices we hear in Banville originate in the interiorised worlds of Joyce and Proust which oppose themselves to a reality that seems brutal, irrational and philistine, and dismiss the fictional illusions of a realism that purports to reflect that order. As David Lodge puts it, when considering these radical forms of fiction: 'There is no point in carefully creating fiction that gives an illusion of life when life itself seems illusory.'[3]

Such a distrust of the inherited or conventional modes of representing reality has a radical effect on the significance and value of plot and language in modern fiction. The result, as Malcolm Bradbury says, 'tends to be a narrative in which there is nothing to narrate except the narrative act itself, an act busily disembarrassing itself of order and causality'.[4] The issue is no longer whether fiction is a worthy alternative to reality, but whether there is any point in writing at all. Such hesitant self-consciousness becomes part of the texture of much post-modernist writing, and is certainly one of the creative hallmarks of Banville's work. Again, David Lodge summarises some of the distinctive ways in which the inheritors of modernism try to resist assimilation into conventional categories of the literary:

> ... combining in one work violently contrasting modes — the obviously fictive and the apparently factual; introducing the author and the question of authorship into the text; and exposing conventions in the act of using them.[5]

Surrounded by literary artifice and convention, the radical novelist has to tread carefully through this hall of mirrors and find images that best express his different sense of purpose. If the old faith is replaced by a new scepticism, then the writer finds, or places, himself in an almost impossible situation, whereby fiction becomes an end in itself, with absolutely no claim to 'truth' or 'reality'; or else it concentrates on its own inadequacies, often trying to forge a new sense of honesty and freedom. If fiction stops trying to pretend to knowledge, then it accepts its own imaginative nature. Post-modernism is based on this kind of radical doubt and acceptance, nowhere more eloquently than in Beckett's haunting work. This kind of fiction lives dangerously, pushing the language of uncertainty to such an extreme that we find it remarkable that the act of writing can continue to survive under such relentless pressure. Beckett's lonely narrators, defiant and nostalgic, comforting themselves with words alone, are a strong and decisive presence in Banville's fiction. Nowhere in modern literature does Lukács's sense of 'a world that has been abandoned by God' find such stylish acceptance.

Banville's fiction contains many elements of both modernist and post-modernist writing, but he has achieved a distinctive style with its own mythology, one that holds together the great humanistic issues of knowledge and imagination. As with Joyce, this kind of narrative draws on a European inheritance for a structure of ideas, genres and images, partly in the belief that literature can write only about itself, but also because such an allusive and symbolic pattern establishes and preserves the dream-like formality of the imaginative dimension. When asked why his novels were so dense with literary and cultural reference, Banville replied:

> We're part of a tradition, a *European* tradition; why not acknowledge it? And then, books are to a large extent made out of other books; why not acknowledge that too? Also, I find that the incorporation of references to other works, and even quotations from those works, gives the text a peculiar and interesting resonance, which is registered even when the reader does not realize that something is being quoted.[6]

Banville, like his narrators, picks his way through the history of imagination, using names, stereotypes, quotations, images and settings, to capture thought and emotion in a pattern that is always memorial. In *Birchwood*, for example, Gabriel Godkin reflects that 'all thinking is in a sense remembering': Banville builds his own house of fiction out of a wealth of recollected figures who, in different ways, have contributed to man's enquiry into the relationships between art and reality, rationalism and idealism, evil and beauty. The rhetorical authority and stylistic grace of Banville's fiction comes from this balanced tension between a classical design, rich and evocative, and a lonesome elegiac voice. All his narrators look back to their origins and their immediate past for some clue to their sense of tragic and farcical confusion. The underlying and enabling myth is, of course, one of lost innocence.

But these tormented narrators are always themselves writers, and thereby Banville closes the fictional circle around them. Without realising it, they hear the voices of a host of other writers—Donne, Proust, Rilke, Shakespeare, Wallace Stevens, Nietzsche, Beckett, Thomas Mann, Nabokov— voices that set up a murmuring tension throughout these retrospective fictions, and whose function, poetically, is to intensify the yearning for imaginative order. The series of novels about the great astronomers goes straight to the heart of the Enlightenment, a movement that both civilised and impoverished perception and understanding. These intellectual voyagers, who open up new worlds to humanity, are impressive, heroic and tragic emblems of lost innocence and alienated knowledge. There is a compassionate strain throughout Banville's work which can celebrate and pity such ambition and vanity, humanise and individualise its inevitable grief and, through the consolations of beauty and nature, offer the willing imagination hope of redemption. This is why most of the novels end with the seasonal hope of spring.

Banville's radical fiction, it turns out, can be quite old-fashioned, or classical, in its affections. But it is too honest simply to romanticise forms of innocence, knowing that the irrationality and violence of human existence precludes any easy comfort. Above all else, childhood remains an obsessive image, a haunting memory for all Banville's protagonists, who try to imagine themselves out of their chaos. Driven by suffering and confusion into fiction and fantasy, they long to retrieve some of the mute wisdom that intellect and language have petrified. In the epigraph to *The Newton Letter*, Banville quotes the astronomer's belated sense of self-understanding:

> I seem to have been only as a boy playing on the seashore, and diverting myself in now and then finding a smoother pebble than ordinary, whilst the great ocean of truth lay all undiscovered before me.

The figure of the child in such fictions provides a powerful psychological dimension, especially in its recurrent form of twins, whereby the divided self, one angelic, the other demonic, can be linked to the major themes of antagonism between reason and imagination, science and art, history and fiction.

Perhaps the most compelling and lyrical version of a child-like state of being is when imaginative perception rediscovers the wonder of the commonplace world. All the great epiphanies in Banville's fiction present us with this sense of unsolicited revelation, a passionate and delightful sense of simple beauty, always there but usually obscured or dismissed by intellect. In a critical sense, Banville's fiction belongs to that Romantic and humanistic protest on behalf of the artist and the imagination against the shackles of rational and speculative thought. At the very same time, however, it is enriched by the humanising purpose of the Enlightenment tradition which encourages questioning and doubt. God may have abandoned the world, but Banville's characters, through intense imaginative effort, can still catch glimpses of an earthly Eden.

If the sublime is forever frustrated by the ridiculous, it seems appropriate that Banville's 'supreme fiction' should return again and again to an Irish cultural experience well stocked with stereotypes.[7] That fiction yearns for some heavenly or imagined order, but it is often forced back to County Wexford. The Irish historical experience includes the near loss of one language and the modern adaptation to another, recurrent political and sectarian violence, an ambiguous sense of cultural loyalty and identity, and an odd, exiled relation with the rest of Europe: such features are classic symptoms of what we may abstractly call 'modern alienation'. A history of political abnormality, linguistic confusion and cultural isolation provides a happy hunting-ground for the post-modernist writer, especially for one like Banville, with such an intelligent sense of humour.

The Big House genre, for example, helps to structure several of the novels—*Birchwood, The Newton Letter, Mefisto, The Book of Evidence*—and provides Banville with a ready-made, strangely familiar cast.[8] A fiction that uses, and parodies, such an institutionalised genre as the Big House, does so in order to set up imaginative expectations which that same fiction must subvert. Banville has tried to explain his attraction to this literary ghost:

> ... in a way it's a huge museum of the past for us. It raises hackles, it raises expectations. No Irish person could be absolutely unmoved for [sic] it.[9]

The reader as well as the fictional character is often led up the garden path by this kind of narrative, eventually finding out, to his mortification, that the reality of the situation is cleverly camouflaged by appearance. Thus, the narrator of *The Newton Letter*, having slipped into a sentimental fantasy about the aristocratic roots of the Lawless family, finds out that they are Catholic, not Protestant. These kinds of deception and illusion depend heavily on, usually Romantic, stereotypes, and are a recurrent fictional game in the novels. Such narrative tricks and trapdoors, here in an Irish context, are easily transferred to the illusory ambitions of the men of science.

The Irish experience also suggests a self-consciousness with regard to language which Banville is ready to exploit in the interests of a narrative always uneasy about the meaning and accuracy of words. A sense of the strangeness of what should be familiar, or even 'natural', characterises the oversensitive consciousness of many of his narrators. Travelling with Prospero's circus around the west of Ireland, Gabriel Godkin is fascinated by the 'strange macaronic talk' in the pubs, just as Freddie Montgomery is struck by the 'bad Irish' spoken by the political prisoners. The historical reality of a fading language, and the novelty of an acquired one, provides Banville (as it did Beckett) with a favoured metaphor for unintelligibility. In a talk delivered to a conference of writers, Banville addressed this ambiguous issue of the English language in Ireland:

> For the Irish, language is not primarily a tool for expressing what we mean. Sometimes I think it is quite the opposite. We have profound misgivings about words. We love them—all too passionately, some of us—but we do not trust them. Therefore we play with them. I am well aware of the danger there is in saying these things. Shamrocks. Leprechauns. The gift of the gab. Little old men with pipes in their gobs sitting on ditches and maundering on about how things were in their fathers' time. In a word, pronounced chaarrm. If I have conjured these images, please banish them at once from your minds. What I am talking about is something subversive, destructive even, and in a way profoundly despairing. Listen to any group of Irish people conversing, from whatever class, in whatever circumstances, and behind the humour and the rhetoric and the slyness you will detect a dark note of hopelessness before the phenomenon of a world that is always *out there*.[10]

Whatever about the historical and linguistic truth behind these observations, ever since Stephen Dedalus's conversation with the dean of studies in *A Portrait of the Artist as a*

Young Man, in which he senses the foreign quality of his own speech, such a felt remove from English has been an important myth in Irish literary culture.

Although Banville has spoken of his own sense of detachment from any idea of a 'national' literature,[11] his Irish background plays a decisive, if unpredictable, role in the fiction. He belongs to what Richard Kearney calls the 'critical counter-tradition' in Irish writing, a radical resistance that includes those novelists—Joyce, Beckett, Flann O'Brien— who make narrative itself the subject of their fictions.[12] This self-conscious narrative, which delights in formal, technical gamesmanship, and which distances itself from realism through symbolism and parody, offers Banville the kind of imaginative freedom that allows him both to imitate and exploit the Irish tradition.

Any Irish writer, but especially one like Banville, is aware of the ways in which Joyce and Beckett negotiated a radical fiction out of their cultural inheritance and artistic ambition. An astute literary critic himself, Banville has pointed to Joyce's 'acceptance' of the everyday world of phenomena as the key to his monumental art,[13] a pleasure in the ordinary sensuous world which finds a most eloquent reformulation in characters like Kepler. Writing about Beckett's novels, Banville has singled out 'the solidity and splendour of their classical base', and their rigorous concentration on 'the moment' in their reflections.[14] The modernist or post-modernist writer in Ireland, trying to avoid conventional pieties while forever lured back to some authentic version of experience, sees that complete artistic freedom from tradition and culture may be the biggest deception of all. One solution is to write in a different kind of language. Joyce and Beckett had done this in a way that allowed the Irish experience to serve as a metaphor for the world, thereby linking the personal with the universal, the provincial with the centre. Both writers offer supreme models, to be learnt from and then overcome, for an art which would be true to itself. Of this inheritance, Banville remarks:

> Modernism has run its course. So also, for that matter, has post-modernism. I believe, at least I hope, that we are on the threshold of a new *ism*, a new synthesis. What will it be? I do not know. But I hope it will be an art which is honest enough to despair and yet go on; rigorous and controlled, cool and yet passionate, without delusions, aware of its own possibilities and its own limits; an art which knows that truth is arbitrary, that reality is multifarious, that language is not a clear lens.
>
> Did I say *new*? What I have defined is as old as Homer.[15]

Banville's own fiction, while intensely self-critical and radically innovative, relishes its attachment to classical forms of modernism. In sharing the remains of modern European literary culture, he pays constant tribute to that culture through allusion, symbol and metaphor. The Irish contribution to that culture must overcome the limits of its own small world but, as the examples of Joyce and Beckett have shown, the provincial often supplies most of the necessary fictions.

A good, and a typically playful example of Banville's deceptive use of the traditional, is revealed by the author himself, while commenting on the fictional influence of his Irish background:

> I had, nor have, none of that loyalty to county which is a characteristic of the Irish. To me, when I lived there, the notion of 'Wexford', and all that the name was supposed to imply, was faintly risible. It was long after I had left that I realised how deeply I was rooted in the place, or how deeply it was rooted in me. All the landscapes of my books are in some way imbued with wexfordness, even when they are supposed to be modern Greece, or medieval Prussia. When I needed to paint a picture of Copernicus's Torun, or Kepler's Weilderstadt, it was Wexford that I conjured up. Now, when a reader tells me how well I captured the Swabia of the seventeenth

century, I smile politely, and hear a ghostly Wexford weasel-voice saying, *Oh him? — sure I knew his oul fella.*[16]

Wexford is as much an invention, it turns out, as Swabia, a landscape of the imagination, composed of images carefully arranged by a sensuous memory.[17] That kind of landscape is truer to the needs of imagination and pure fiction than any 'realistic' version because it recaptures the world of sensation and perception and exemplifies the dream-like quality of remembrance. This kind of Proustian past has to be invented because it has to be invested with some meaningful pattern.

Banville's fictional aesthetic, while it welcomes the presence and spirit of many great modern writers, has its own distinctive shape and purposeful tone. It is a richly eclectic fiction committed to the idea of a transcendent humanistic ethic. The form of his novels, at their best, is simple yet ingenious, the style densely metaphoric. His own favourite analogy for the kind of novel he tries to create is that of a poeticised dream, in which a single voice, through a persuasive and coherent tone, controls the chaos of recollection.[18] To orchestrate that kind of effect stylistically, requires great technical and formal care. But Banville's fiction is rarely answerable to the charge of being simply learned or aridly clever, as is the case with much post-modernist fiction written by novelists living too close to theory.[19] Here, technique serves a passionate utterance in which imaginative perception can reclaim some sense of a human and humanising order, while accepting confusion with good grace.

Herbert Marcuse has spoken of the utopian nostalgia evident in great literature, in fictions which translate the present into a dream of the past in order to better imagine a future:

> In this remembrance, art has recognized what is and what could be, within and beyond the social conditions. Art has rescued this knowledge from the sphere of abstract concept and embedded it in the realm of

sensuousness. Its cognitive power draws its strength from this realm. The sensuous force of the Beautiful keeps the promise alive—memory of the happiness that once was, and that seeks its return.[20]

Banville's fiction is essentially based on this tension between the abstract and the sensuous, between those modes of understanding and perception such as language, which conceal reality, and those, like the images of a waking dream, which restore humanity to its senses.

1

Long Lankin

> The role of objects, is to restore silence.
> Samuel Beckett, *Molloy*

JOHN BANVILLE'S first published work, *Long Lankin* (1970), is an unusual assembly of fictions. It is arranged in two parts: part one is a series of nine short stories, part two, 'The Possessed', is a novella. The title of the collection is taken from an old Scots–English ballad, 'Long Lankin' or 'Lamkin', the story of a horrific murder. Intent on revenge against a former master, Long Lankin steals into the house while the master is away and, with the help of a treacherous nurse, sadistically murders the baby of the house:

> 'Where's the little heir of this house?' said Long Lankin.
> 'He's asleep in his cradle', said the false nurse to him.
> 'We'll prick him, we'll prick him all over with a pin,
> And that'll make my lady to come down to him.'

The mother hears the screams of the baby and the appeal from the nurse, and is lured to her own murder:

> My lady came down, she was thinking no harm
> Long Lankin stood ready to catch her in his arm.
> Here's blood in the kitchen. Here's blood in the hall.
> Here's blood in the parlour where my lady did fall.

It is a shocking tale of calculated cruelty and ritual slaughter, all the more horrific because there is scant evidence of any motive for such evil.[1]

None of Banville's stories deals directly with the character of Long Lankin. Instead, he uses the violent pattern of the legend to structure and unify a series of stories set in contemporary Ireland. The tale of Long Lankin is used to create and sustain an atmosphere of foreboding and anxiety for a series of psychological fictions. All the stories, and the novella, re-enact the drama of Long Lankin's violent and cruel intrusion. Banville himself has commented on his original intention:

> The stories, all nine stories, have each a cast of two characters closely involved with each other—they are in love, they are married, they hate each other, whatever—whose relationship is destroyed, or disturbed in some radical way, by the interference of a third character, the Long Lankin, or interloper, figure.[2]

The imaginative intention is clear and dramatic. How effectively, though, is the original horror story translated into a modern psychological form?

The opening story, 'Wild Wood', is one of the most successful evocations of the kind of primitive mystery and fear suggested by the ballad. Two boys have mitched from school and sit by a fire in a wood. One of them, called Horse, 'a strange wild creature who rarely spoke and never smiled', cuts wood for the fire with an axe. Suddenly a third boy appears and tells them of the savage murder of an old woman-shopkeeper, the climax of a violent intrusion in which, mysteriously, nothing was stolen. Horse listens but says nothing. Then, leaving his axe by the fire, he walks off into the wood, leaving the two frightened boys alone with the echo of their calls. It is a carefully told story, dependent on mystery and suggestion for its eerie effect. The brooding character of Horse, the primitive setting, the implied connection between Horse's axe and the inexplicable murder—these are the main elements of a convincing atmospheric tale. Most effective is the suggestion that behind 'Wild Wood' lies a story withheld.

As with Joyce's *Dubliners*, there is in *Long Lankin* a clear sense of stylistic purpose and conscious formal arrangement.[3] Banville's stories, however, do not foreground a social or political condition. They are more concerned with the psychology of fear: these are studies in melancholia. Such an existential condition does not lend itself easily to dramatisation, and several of the stories, however carefully written, merely contrive or assert despair and dread without creating a convincing dramatic situation.

Two of the most convincing stories are 'The Visit' and 'Summer Voices', both of which deal with childhood. The first of these is about the fragile freedom offered by imagination. A small girl living with an old aunt waits anxiously for a promised visit from her long absent father. While waiting, she encounters a travelling magician named Rainbird who delights her with fabulous tricks and then takes her for a hair-rising spin on his bicycle. She returns to the house for the expected visit, now determined not to see her father, but is dragged screaming to pay her respects. The primitive emotions of this story have a dramatic and psychological coherence uncomplicated by the brooding consciousness of other stories in the collection. Rainbird, the unexpected intruder, represents a delightful form of imaginative release from the tension of ambivalent expectation. The father, paradoxically, becomes an unwelcome and sinister intruder. The same girl reappears in 'Summer Voices', this time with a brother. The two set off from their aunt's house to keep a secret appointment with an old man who has promised to show them a corpse washed up by the sea. The girl savours the grotesque surprise as much as she enjoys her brother's fear. Once they get home and prepare to go to bed, the recollected image of the corpse suddenly terrifies the girl, and she pleads for the brother's comfort and physical reassurance. He coldly ignores her and she goes to bed alone, terrified and weeping. The boy's earlier humiliation is revenged. The sinister quality in these two stories comes partly from the blend of cruelty and innocence. As we shall see later, there is always something creepy about Banville's children: more like malevolent dwarfs than sweet young things.

The novella that follows the short stories, 'The Possessed', is a tale of existential suffering. It is prefaced by an epigraph taken from André Gide's *L'Immoraliste*:

16   *John Banville: A Critical Study*

> Take me away from here and give
> me some reason for living. I
> have none left. I have freed myself.
> That may be. But what does it signify?
> This objectless liberty is a burden to me.[4]

Just as the legend of Long Lankin serves as a symbolic structure for the stories, these lines from Gide, we may assume, give notice of the existential dilemma at the heart of 'The Possessed'. The first thing we may note about this novella is the reappearance of many characters from the short stories. The central character, Ben White, a writer, has already appeared in 'Island'; as have Jacob and Norman Collins in 'Persona', Julie and Helen in 'Sanctuary', and Morris and Liza in 'Nightwind'. More significantly, Ben appears here with a sister, Flora, and their relationship is clearly a development of the incestuous passion hinted at in 'Summer Voices'. 'The Possessed' functions as a kind of emotional showdown for the characters introduced in the short stories.

The story is set in the wealthy home of Liza and Morris Gold who are hosting a party for their friends. Ben, just back from a holiday in Greece, acts as the interloper in this situation, and his unexpected arrival triggers off a series of bizarre, often violent, incidents which characterise this piece of intellectual Gothic. As the final summary reworking of the Long Lankin tale, we may see the Golds as versions of the lord and lady of the house, Flora as the criminal accomplice and Ben as the agent of tragedy.

From the start, Ben is determined to provoke trouble among this middle-class gathering. His first victim is Colm, a young earnest accountant, who arrives at the party with Flora. Colm despises the social pretensions of the party, and is particularly hostile to the blatant theatricality of a homosexual called Wolf. This encounter produces a defence and explanation by Wolf of what he calls the 'displaced persons set':

> There is no great meaning and no great unified truth to

strive after. There are only little bits and pieces. Little broken things to pick up and play with. Things that can never be reassembled. Your fine upstanding world made sure that nothing could ever be reassembled once you had it broken.

He paused, and his face relaxed into a smile. — And still you carry on the old lies, he went on, a dull edge of weariness in his voice. You make rules and morals and politics and gods and then you have the nerve to turn around and offer them as proofs that you are real and that a kind and personal god watches over you. That you are right and anyone who disagrees with you is lost. The awful thing is Colm that anyone who has the foolishness to disagree is indeed lost because you own the world. But for tonight you are alone and we have you in our corner. So friend prepare to suffer a little bit. (125–6)

This is a defence of decadence, all the more passionate because it is delivered in the presence of outraged bourgeois morality. Like parts of Banville's fiction itself, the purpose is to shock and discomfort. Its studied contempt for conventional morality and respectability comes, outwardly at least, from those who embody both. Bored with security and money, they search for some spiritual passion to enliven their empty lives. Characters like Wolf are not the most convincing or sympathetic medium for an exposure of the imaginative dullness of middle-class society. But sympathy has little or no place in this kind of fiction which, like its characters, prefers the dramatic effects of outrageous gestures to the banalities of conventional wisdom about the world. One such piece of theatricality is the recitation of 'Long Lankin' by one of the guests, Jacob, to the assembled company, a performance which reflects and intensifies the growing tension at the party.

The central episode of the novella is devoted to the escapades of Ben and Flora, who leave the party and drive around Dublin all night in a series of phantasmagoric incidents. The purpose of this part of the story is to create an image of a surreal underworld, typified by encounters with strange grotesque figures like the man with a car full of souvenir leprechauns or the alcoholic who carries around a public telephone in his pocket. The only scene in this part which retains any coherent link with the theme of the story is where Flora taunts Ben with her sexuality, reminding him of their childhood passion. Ben recalls the incident behind 'Summer Voices':

> Some day I shall be drowned. From the rails of a ship at midnight or on the sunlit beach that sea will take me. That one that was lost and they took him out after a week. I recognised something in that ruined face. You laughed at the sight but I saw some rumour of the future. (157)

However clear the link with an earlier story, episodes like this become increasingly dislocated from the dramatic continuity and coherence of 'The Possessed'. Ben's utterances remain deliberately cryptic. Even Flora wearies of his studied portentousness, remarking, 'Ben, I'm tired of you and your beautiful pain.' Once back at the party, Ben asks Jacob to explain 'Long Lankin' to him:

> —It's a weird song you know, he said. I got it from a fellow when I was doing that job over in Sussex. Long Lankin. Aye.
> Ben waited, and when nothing more came he asked—What is it about Jacob? What's it supposed to mean?—Ah there was a notion in the old days that a leper could cure himself if he murdered someone and caught the blood in a silver cup. Innocent blood do you see. Maybe Lankin was a leper. I don't know. (174–5)

This is a predictable anticlimax to a fiction that makes a virtue of world-weariness. The problem is that, stylistically and dramatically, the story suffers badly from its chronic seriousness, its cultivated *angst*: mystery becomes obscurity, the prophetic becomes pretentious, and the initial declaration of philosophical ambition becomes a burdensome rationale for the bizarre actions of characters. Ben is more like an intellectual thug than a tormented soul.

At the end of the story, Ben confides to Mrs Gold his envy of the Greek communists—'They had a cause. They believed in things.' Now that the night of reckoning is over, he voices his ambition as a writer in search of similar force of conviction:

> ... I think I might write a book. I could tell a story about the stars and what it's like all alone up there. He looked into the sky, but there were no stars, and he smiled at her and said—I musn't feel sorry for myself. And anyway there are all kinds of things I could do. Join a circus maybe. (188)

These two images of escape, in reverse order, provide Banville with important metaphors for much of his subsequent fiction.

Looking back on *Long Lankin*, Banville himself is not very sentimental:

> The novella in *Long Lankin* is ghastly, absolutely dreadful ... I like the stories in *Long Lankin*. I kept the style as bare as I could, and kept speculations of inner motives to a minimum.[5]

In 1984, fourteen years after its original appearance, *Long Lankin* was republished by Banville,[6] who had chosen to substitute a different short story entitled 'De Rerum Natura' for 'Persona', the concluding piece of part one, and to withhold 'The Possessed' completely. Without the novella, the collection of short stories seems simpler, less pretentious, more coherent. 'De Rerum Natura', taking its title from Lucretius's poem in praise of pleasure,[7] centres on an old man who has withdrawn into the garden of his dilapidated home, consumed with delight at the intensity of nature's fertility. His pleasure is interrupted by a visit from his confused and guilty son and an outraged daughter-in-law. Uncompromisingly 'natural', the old man finally seduces the son into staying with him, while the woman, scandalised, leaves the pair to their primitive fantasy. This tale of the imagination rejuvenated by nature provides an effective coda to a sequence of stories about man's distorted nature.

Why was 'The Possessed' excluded in the new edition? I suggest that the author felt that the novella complicated the taut shape of the collection and that it was, artistically, too self-indulgent. A more mature Banville has commented on this problem of style and audience:

> It's foolish to expect readers to take you as seriously as you do yourself. Just because you've spent years of your life on something, doesn't mean you should expect them to treat it with due solemnity. They're more frivolous than that—thank God.[8]

Banville's literary sense of irony, often aimed at himself, should warn us to discriminate between earnestness and seriousness.

Long Lankin is a difficult work, but it shows serious and skilled talent in the apprentice. These are experimental sketches for larger canvasses to come. The enduring idea in *Long Lankin* is that of the writer himself, in search of an imagery and a form that will represent his sense of the mysteriousness of reality.

2
Nightspawn

> Is the view of nature and of social relations on which the Greek imagination and hence Greek mythology is based possible with self-acting mule spindles and railways and locomotives and electrical telegraphs? What chance has Vulcan against Roberts & Co., Jupiter against the lightningrod and Hermes against the Crédit Mobilier?
>
> Karl Marx, *Grundrisse*

NIGHTSPAWN (1971) is a psychological thriller about political espionage in modern Greece. As with *Long Lankin*, however, the genre and setting are not part of a realistic purpose. The thriller genre offers a plot involving some of Banville's favoured motifs—mystery, pursuit, confusion of identities and the need to find a solution to the pattern of events described. The exotic setting of the Greek islands allows a superficial exploitation of mythology, mostly that of names for characters, in order to provide some philosophical and literary structure to the tale. Stylistically, a certain degree of superficiality is attractive to such a playful formalist as Banville. This is especially true of a writer who distrusts the purpose and conventions of a more realistic fiction. In this case, as in later fictions, Banville aims at psychological, not social realism. The chosen genre plays the part of a dramatic metaphor. As a recent study has pointed out, this is often the case with modern writers who turn to the formulaic conventions of such a popular genre:

> The spy thriller is ostensibly one of the most 'political' of popular ficton genres. Its subject is global politics: the Empire, fascism, communism, the Cold War, terrorism. Yet its political subject is only a pretext to the adventure formulas and the plots of betrayal, disguise, and doubles which are at the heart of the genre and of the reader's investment.[1]

Not surprisingly, however, there is a strong parodic element in Banville's version of the thriller. Stereotypes, precisely because they are so 'far-fetched', so endearingly unreal, will always attract Banville's purely fictive intention.

Nightspawn is told by Ben White, the central character of 'The Possessed'. As we shall see, the choice of a tormented writer as a narrator helps to explain many of the formal difficulties, the depth and the narcissism of this novel. His mournful tale seems largely the product of his obsessive character which is presented in the opening lines:

> I am a sick man, I am a spiteful man. I think my life is diseased. Only a flood of spleen now could cauterize my wounds. This is it. Hear the slap and slither of the black tide rising. The year has blundered through another cycle, and another summer has arrived, bringing the dog rose to the hedge, the clematis swooning to the door. The beasts are happily ravening in the sweltering fields of June. How should I begin? Should I say that the end is inherent in every beginning? My hyacinth is dead, and will never bloom again, but I keep the pot, like Isabella, and water with my tears in vain the torn and withered roots. What else is there for me to do? They took everything from me. Everything.[2]

This darkly cryptic opening, with its strange mixture of melodrama and romance, its allusions to Dostoyevsky and Keats,[3] puts into perspective the kind of contradictory narrative we may expect. *Nightspawn* is a fiction about a story difficult to tell, impossible to fully understand, but necessary to write. Greece, once the heart of classical culture, is now the post-modernist setting for a corrupted, nostalgic imagination.

Ben begins his tale by recalling his solitary arrival on the Greek islands, where he meets Erik Weiss and a companion, Andreas, a strange pair of grotesques. Weiss, a political journalist, is 'a tall gangling creature' with 'fearsome yellow teeth ... marooned like crooked tombstones in the midst of an awkward mouth'. Andreas is a 'dark Greek gentleman with a handsome face, furious eyes, and a hideously crooked back'. White wants to join forces with these two bizarre conspirators because, as he puts it, 'accidie was my greatest fear'. Political drama in a world of decisive action promises him some relief from existential boredom: becoming a revolutionary agent might provide him with something to believe in. As soon becomes clear, however, the possibility of such action seems as obscure and unreal as everything else in his life. Waiting for something to happen, Ben encounters the Kyd family, Julian, a wealthy Englishman, his Greek wife Helena, and son Yacinth. Tired of waiting for his conspirators, he has a violent, passionate and farcical affair with Helena. He also tries to make friends with Yacinth, who silently ignores him. Julian, Ben discovers, is also conspiring with the Greek military. The recollected plot becomes increasingly confused and confusing. Erik is murdered for betraying secrets, Andreas seeks revenge for Erik, and Ben soon realises that he is only a pawn in a complex game of shifting loyalties. He recalls trying to murder Julian, accidentally killing Yacinth, and finally taking secret refuge when the military coup takes place. He leaves the island with none of the expected pursuers on his trail. Once he recovers some peace, he begins to write *Nightspawn*.

Such a summary of events is, like Banville's intention, deceptive. An important part of the story's meaning lies not with its contrived anti-plot, but with the mind of the narrator. More precisely, the dominant theme of the novel is the problem and burden of fiction itself. The work begins with a conviction, based on experience, of the unreliability of narrative conventions and the uselessness of commitment. It deliberately chooses a political genre to prove the inevitability of both failures. Banville is frank about the aim of the book: 'In *Nightspawn* I set out to fail. What was important was the *quality* of that failure.'[4] Nothing could express more clearly the self-imposed paradoxical aim of such a post-modernist fiction. It is an ingenious ambition which defies realistic gravity, but which also requires new convincing illusions.

A parodic thriller seems an appropriate form of imaginative contempt for the ideological aspirations of political idealism. On this aspect of *Nightspawn*, Seamus Deane observes that such a self-fulfilling fiction shows a deep disillusion, 'especially with the very idea basic to most politics — that the world is subject to improvement if not to change or transformation'.[5] It is as if Banville sets up Ben White as the Hamlet-type artist desperate to test his character in the public world, and then creates a plot which mirrors the madness of such a venture in order to reassert the superior truths of a private imaginary world.

There are imaginative compensations within such a determinedly fatalistic view, and *Nightspawn* begins to define and explore many of the characteristic features of Banville's special kind of fiction. One such constant feature is the self-consciousness of its narrators. This is a novel about a novelist trying to write a novel. We are continually reminded by Ben that he is composing, editing, lying, inventing, dreaming and memorising. In this way, Banville, through Ben, tests the many fictions of the novel form, and defies its silent assumptions by broadcasting them. He himself has described his method in this novel as 'a kind of betrayal of ... the novelist's guild and its secret signs and stratagems'.[6] The arrogant narrator also enjoys teasing and provoking readers, as well as critics eager for arcane significance, those 'panting hunters of the symbol'. The expectant reader becomes part of the parody. This kind of self-consciousness keeps drawing attention to the medium of the fiction, language itself, as a habit and an inheritance. Repeated interruption of the narrative, whereby the medium as well as its supposed object of reference become a theme in themselves, has a disconcerting honesty which it substitutes for false promises. By denying himself any absolute knowledge, understanding or even talent, the narrator offers an alternative fiction of authenticity. This is a delicate game for any writer to play. It has a serious point to make, but such frankness is no substitute for a persuasive fiction, self-conscious or not.

The most effective fiction within this fiction is of a writer struggling with the disorder of memory. Ben tries to recall the past accurately, but language never seems to serve his memory faithfully:

> I am talking about the past, about remembrance. You find no answers, only questions. It is enough, almost enough. That day I thought about the island, and now I think about thinking about the island, and tomorrow, tomorrow I shall think about thinking about thinking about the island, and all will be one, however I try, and there will be no separate thoughts, but only one thought, one memory, and I shall still know nothing. What am I talking about, what are these ravings? About the past, of course, and about Mnemosyne, that lying whore. And I am talking about torment. (113)

Mnemosyne, as the Greek personification of memory, plays cruel tricks with Ben's imagination: as mother of the Muses, she plays havoc with his attempt to write it down. Most of the self-conscious effects in Ben's narrative come from this sense that the book he is trying to write is doomed. Language and its literary conventions sound like a poor, usually farcical, reproduction of an experience beyond words. As Ben remarks, 'Art is, after all, only mimicry'. Parody is, predictably, the natural expression of this painful and laughable sense of disjunction between an original and a copy.

But within the overall parody, Ben insists on the need to reinvent a past that cannot be reproduced. Again and again, descriptive passages occur in *Nightspawn* which first ask to be taken seriously, and are then exposed as a contrivance on the part of the writer to impose meaning and emotion where none was felt. For example, after a scene which recalls the growing tenderness and intimacy between Ben and Helena, we read:

> O Jesus, I can reproduce no more of this twaddle. Did she really say all that, and expect me to take her

> seriously? It seems incredible. And yet, what am I saying? I took her seriously, indeed I did. (93)

Once deflation is recognised as the favoured irony of this anti-novel, then it becomes difficult to know what or whom to take seriously. Despite its self-mockery and the games it plays with the reader, *Nightspawn* is certainly trying to say something authentic about love and grief. Although not always dramatised convincingly, the novel's ploys amount to a view of narrative as metaphor. Caught, like Beckett's narrators, between the urge to write and the foreknowledge of such a crafty deception, this strange narrative defends its form as something 'no better than these vague suggestions, this mixed bag of metaphors'.

This kind of fiction has an answer, or an excuse, for everything. The story fails, so the logic goes, because it was intended to. Nothing is resolved, because that would be a lie. Descriptions are always misleading, because they suggest a faith and understanding which were never there originally. Banville's first experimental novel deliberately makes life very difficult for itself. Yet it obviously taught Banville important lessons about the kind of fiction he wanted to create—'Certainly it has terrible faults—its clumsiness, for instance, and its false intellectual bravado—yet I am very fond of that book, because I think it is, in a way, the most honest thing I have done.'[7] It should be said, despite the self-indulgent nature of the novel, that there is much here of enduring significance for Banville's later fiction. Early on in the story, in one of its most characteristic passages, the ultimate value of the fictional experiment is anticipated:

> How tedious this is. Could I not take it all as understood, the local colour and quaint customs, and then get on to the real meat of things? But I suppose the conventions must be observed. And anyway, there are pearls here strewn among this sty of words. (36)

Nightspawn may be, in places, a 'sty of words', but the 'pearls' represent the novelist's need for faith and consolation.

If politics provides the necessary nightmare, then romance offers the possibility of momentary comfort. Both the conspiracy and the love-affair end in tragedy, but Ben's supposed love for Helena creates a lyrical tension in his story which accounts for the nostalgic tone of much of the narrative. In keeping with the conventions of the romance-thriller, personal freedom and desire are usually overwhelmed by political intrigue and corruption. Ben is afraid of romanticising his affair with Helena, and so we have a romance plot as confusing and unpredictable as that of the thriller. Love is not exempt from evil and illusion. We are given a version of the past in which no character's true identity or relation with others can be stated with any certainty. From such a conviction, everything and everyone must be reinvented in such a way as to confirm that sceptical faith.

Ben's inclination to romanticise his past with Helena is regularly subverted by his cynical disillusionment:

> O yes, I knew my part well, the gay pirate with a cutlass in his teeth, laughing heartily in the face of the king and his justice. What a fool, what an incredible fool. I kissed her mouth to silence her, and soon we were making violent and lunging love, causing the bed, the window panes, the very walls to rattle. But afterwards, that sadness returned, and we lay captive in a fearful silence, our wide eyes watching the light grow in the window. (129)

Ben's retrospective image of himself as chivalric hero pitting his love against the world of power is a bitter piece of self-parody. Aside from the rare suggestion of real achieved intimacy in the above quotation, most of his memories of love are reconstructions of poor theatre, best expressed through ludicrous stereotypes. All the conventional expressions of romantic love make him wish 'there were better ways of expressing that ancient lie'.

In fact, the plot acknowledges that Ben had been lying to himself about the real object of his desire. He discovers that Helena is Julian's daughter, not his wife. Horrified by this disclosure, or seeming to be so, he does not deny that his true passion was for the boy, Yacinth. Incest, adultery and forbidden love are the secretive forms of lust which lie below appearance and language. We may recall that at the beginning of his tale, Ben confesses, 'My hyacinth is dead, and will never bloom again.' The myth of the beautiful Greek youth, Hyacinthus, was first used in 'The Possessed', when Wolf told the story to Ben as an allegory of freedom and jealousy. Here it is blended with the legend of Isabella, from Keats's version of Boccaccio's story, in which the distraught mistress seeks to preserve the severed head of her murdered lover by watering it with her tears.[8] The motif of incest was also at the centre of 'The Possessed', in the relationship between Ben and Flora.

Why this preoccupation with myth, legend and forbidden forms of desire? I think it reflects Banville's need to explore emotions and beliefs beyond the reach or influence of social or literary convention. It suggests an eclectic imagination, ready to use any available literary image, from unfamiliar legend to well-worn stereotype, to create a fiction that always acknowledges its own contrivances. It can often result in an extravagant form of writing, melodramatic and grotesque, part of a desire to shock and be shocked.

Though *Nightspawn* suffers from what Ben himself calls his 'self-congratulatory sense of alienation', this confessional novel has a clearly recognisable form of modern protest at its core. It is a cry against the corruption of the human spirit by time and circumstance. In one of the few passages in the novel where the serious expression of belief is not immediately mocked by a narrator embarrassed by earlier foolishness, Ben defines the nature of this sense of generalised loneliness:

'Isn't it strange how all these things work together', I mused. 'The wind lifts the waves, and the waves pound the shore. These strange cycles. People too, with their cycles and reversals that cause so much anguish. It's amazing.'

I looked at Erik. Erik looked at the sea. I went on, 'Imitating the seasons, I suppose. The rages and storms, the silences. If only the world would imitate us once in a while. That would be something, wouldn't it? But the world maintains a contemptuous silence, and what the heart desires, the world is incapable of giving.' (102)

Romantic lyricism and reflection like this come as a bit of a surprise in a story narrated by such a gloomy sceptic as Ben. But this note of infinitely fragile hope is what distinguishes so much of Banville's fiction. It is one of those 'pearls' which prevents despair from turning into absolute silence. In the above quotation, alienated man envies the mysterious order and beauty of the natural world, always being reminded by such a pattern of his own poverty.

Only briefly in *Nightspawn* does Banville create and hold a compelling fiction of this sense of human sadness. Such estrangement is occasionally consoled by an invented and imaginative order of beauty and harmony, comparable, but inferior, to nature—in other words, where the artist rewrites experience to defy time and circumstance. After the violent experimentation of *Nightspawn*, Banville's next novel was to find a way of maintaining its desired fictional purity while conveying a most moving and compassionate tale without fictional embarrassment.

3
Birchwood

> The Past, then, is a constant accumulation of images. It can be easily contemplated and listened to, tested and tasted at random, so that it ceases to mean the orderly alternation of linked events that it does in the large theoretical sense. It is now a generous chaos out of which the genius of total recall ... can pick anything he pleases.
>
> Vladimir Nabokov, Ada

AFTER *Long Lankin* and *Nightspawn*, the most striking features of Banville's next novel, *Birchwood* (1973), are its formal discipline and its refinement of a poetic style. The imaginative setting changes from the modern or contemporary world to nineteenth-century Ireland, and uses the 'Big House' genre to tell a story about the mysterious nature of identity and knowledge. The historical or social accuracy of the period is not the primary issue here. Banville seems to have chosen this well-known genre and its conventions for their imaginative, metaphorical possibilities, their instant associations with decay, political crisis and, significantly, the image of a class of people increasingly out of touch with reality:

> Obviously I was thinking of Carleton, Somerville and Ross, but no one book in particular. I took stock characters, you know, the overbearing father, long-suffering mother, sensitive son, and then also other strands, the quest, the lost child, the doppelgänger.[1]

The Big House genre provides a fictional setting and familiar types, but within this scheme Banville has contrived a plot which draws on the conventions of the romance and its cousin, the thriller.[2] The self-conscious artificiality of the form has, as we shall see, a purpose that is central to the meaning of *Birchwood*. The novel has a fictional rather than a realistic logic of its own, because its narrator can only comprehend and order reality through a subjective imagination.

Like *Nightspawn*, *Birchwood* is a fiction about invention. Its narrator, Gabriel Godkin, is trying to write the story of his childhood in an attempt to understand how the past has led him to his present isolation and confusion. Although he acknowledges the difficulty, sometimes the impossibility, of recalling the past honestly, he tries to give his childhood some retrospective significance. Above all, he wants and needs to understand his mysterious relationship with his family. Godkin's entire account is characterised by a self-conscious tension between a need to relate the facts of a complex past, and the awareness that writing transforms that past into a fiction:

> We imagine that we remember things as they were, while in fact all we carry into the future are fragments which reconstruct a wholly illusory past.[3]

But such a conviction about the limitations, even the futility, of setting memory against the tricks of time, does not prevent Godkin from continuing his memoirs. Past experience may be beyond understanding, but may also, as a solution and a consolation, be reinvented. His story is an imaginative version of the facts, measured and arranged according to the dictates of perception and desire.

Gabriel begins with the history of his family. This opening section of the novel is entitled 'The Book of the Dead', an allusion to the mortuary verses left with the bodies of the Egyptian dead to help them through the afterlife, and to ensure their salvation through a triumph over time.[4] Only by the end of Gabriel's story will we see the significance of this mythical gesture. The family tree, as he says himself, 'is a curious one'. Sometime in the distant past, his great-great grandfather, also called Gabriel Godkin, managed to take over the house and estate which had belonged to the Lawless family for generations. The Lawlesses fought, unsuccessfully, to regain possession, but eventually Gabriel's father, Joseph, married Beatrice Lawless, and Birchwood seemed secured for the Godkins. Because of the family's 'congenital craziness', mismanagement of the estate, 'bled white by agents and gombeen men', and rising peasant rebellion, the estate falls into decay.

In the dilapidated mansion, inhabited by a neurotic father, a disappointed mother and eccentric grandparents, the young Gabriel withdraws into the silent world of 'attics and cellars', his 'favourite haunts'. One day, Aunt Martha, his father's sister, arrives with her son, Michael, 'this virago and her cretin', and the two boys develop a strange reluctant intimacy. Gabriel suddenly decides that he has a lost sister, Rose, whom he is determined to find. With both grandparents dead, with the spread of grotesque and farcical incidents, and the estate besieged by an increasingly daring peasantry, the boy leaves home. Soon after leaving, he encounters and joins a travelling circus, composed of an exotic group of people including two sets of twins. Silas, the head of these colourful nomads, gives Gabriel the 'outlandish alias' of 'Johann Livelb'.[5] With a new identity, travelling around Ireland with his adoptive family, he enjoys an unprecedented sense of imaginative freedom. Then famine strikes. The troupe is pursued by hunger and the authorities, and the adventure ends in death and disaster. Once more Gabriel escapes, only to return to Birchwood. In his absence, the Lawlesses have been slaughtered by the Molly Maguires, 'bands of savage-fanged hermaphrodites', and the estate is now desolate. The sole survivor, Gabriel encounters Michael, now one of the Molly Maguires, and suddenly realises they are twin-brothers, the incestuous sons of Joseph Godkin and his sister, Martha. After this recognition, Michael vanishes. Gabriel takes up a solitary beleaguered residence in the old house, and starts to write his account of 'the fall and rise of Birchwood'.

Through this complex plot of pursuit, mystery and

revelation, Gabriel recreates his past. It is a story that exploits all the stereotypes and conventions of the Big House genre as well as more anachronistic forms and motifs, a tale of terrible irrational destruction and slaughter, told in such a way as to expurgate the horror of those memories, but also to insist on the occasional moments of happiness and beauty during that ordeal. It is also a narrative in which symbolic image, rather than empirical fact, is to be cherished and valued. In the end, such an account manages to explain everything and yet the original sense of mystery is as strong as ever:

> All that blood! That slaughter! And for what? For the same reason that Papa released his father into the birch wood to die, that Granny Godkin tormented poor mad Beatrice, that Beatrice made Martha believe that Michael was in the burning shed, the same reason that brought about all their absurd tragedies, the reason which does not have a name. So here then is an ending, of a kind, to my story. It may not have been like that, any of it. I invent, necessarily. (174)

The story's strangeness, its self-conscious manner, its superficial resolution which concludes the search for a meaning, but does not and cannot comprehend its significance—all these formal elements are stylistic devices to dramatise Gabriel's unique kind of perception, his troubled sense of language's reliability, and his desperate need for an imaginative order to set against the chaos of experience.

In *Birchwood*, for the first time, Banville has found a form and style that convey the 'necessity' of fiction in a dramatically convincing manner. Godkin reinvents the past in such a way as to satisfy his need for emotional and imaginative consolation without denying the horrors of existence. He recreates a nightmare but still believes in the value of 'those extraordinary moments when the pig finds the truffle embedded in the muck'. This metaphor of unexpected magic expresses the kind of tension behind Godkin's degrading but sometimes rewarding quest for beauty and harmony. In *Birchwood*, the beautiful is almost overwhelmed by the grotesque, but remains the only image of hope which eases the pain of recollection.

Gabriel's memory of his childhood is measured by occasional moments of imaginative insight into the nature of a beauty constantly menaced by violence and cruelty. One of the novel's most haunting symbols, an image that holds a morbid fascination for the young boy, is the birch wood itself:

> Our wood was one of nature's cripples. It covered, I suppose, three or four acres of the worst land on the farm, a hillside sloping down crookedly to the untended nether edge of the stagnant pond we called a lake. Under a couple of feet of soil there was a bed of solid rock, that intractable granite for which the area is notorious. On this unfriendly host the trees grew wicked and deformed, some of them so terribly twisted that they crawled horizontally across the hill, their warped branches warring with the undergrowth, while behind them, at some distance, the roots they had struggled to put down were thrust up again by the rock, queer maimed things. Here too, on the swollen trunks, were lymphatic mushrooms flourishing in sodden moss, and other things, reddish glandular blobs which I called dwarfs' ears. It was a hideous, secretive and exciting place, I liked it there, and when, surfeited on the fetid air of the lower wood, I sought the sunlight above the hill, there on a high ridge, to lift my spirit, was the eponymous patch of birches, restless gay little trees which sang in summer, and in winter winds rattled together their bare branches as delicate as lace. (31)

This animistic image, elaborate and detailed, is a curious blend of the lyrical and the horrific. For the boy, this distortion of nature has a contradictory fascination because it pleases his sense of fantasy and mystery. Every detail is a sensuous part of a vision of nature fighting against conventional beauty and arrangement, a primitive rhapsody of defiance and struggle. The climax of the description, however, is an image of transcendent beauty, in lyrical opposition to the nightmarish underworld. The 'gay little trees', 'as delicate as lace,' afford a kind of visual and emotional relief to the perverse and demented forms of nature which threaten but do not reach the summit. The boy's imagination turns instinctively towards the darker forms, as if they hold some vital inexpressible secret not available to reason.

The image of the wood may be read as a reflected image of the subconscious, dream-like mind, seeking comfort in the unreal. Just as Gabriel recalls his love of attics and cellars as his favourite haunts in the house, so too does the silent sinister world of the wood allow him to relive some primitive, almost forbidden, desire. At the beginning of his story, Gabriel wonders, 'what, for instance, did I do in the womb, swimming in those dim red waters with my past time still all before me?' The principal images of *Birchwood* point towards birth and childhood as the profoundest source of later mystery and confusion, dramas around which Banville creates a mythology of ambiguous identity.

Twins are the central motif in this drama of origin and development. Gabriel's story is a re-enactment of his discovery, based on intuition rather than knowledge, that his cousin Michael is his incestuous twin-brother. Looking back, he realises that he invented a fictional sister, and undertook a search for her, in order to deny the existence of this forbidden relationship. As far as the facts are concerned, there was a purpose, however perverse, to the incestuous union between Martha and Joseph: their children would be Godkins, and the Lawless threat to reclaim the property would be legally overcome. Beatrice was barren, and Aunt Martha supplied a future for inheritance through her 'two-card trick'. The presence of twins intensifies the conflict within the Godkin family, a family already suffering from 'congenital craziness'. Which one would inherit the estate? Joseph and Martha had agreed that Gabriel would be the resident heir, but that Michael would eventually be the real one. Martha sensed, rightly, that her brother would secretly alter the will, and the dispossessed son began his merciless revenge.

The point of this scheme is to show how nature, unpredictable and ironic, played havoc with human intention. Gabriel realises now that his parents 'made the wrong choices, and thereby came their ruin'. The oppressive sense of determined fates in *Birchwood* has its psychological roots in forbidden desires which yield a permanent feeling of ambiguity and distortion.

The twin-relationship between Gabriel and Michael also allows Banville to suggest a delicate and intuitive intimacy of opposites, a relationship in which Gabriel can watch himself outside himself. Only now does Gabriel suggest that Michael's arrival at Birchwood threatened him in some way— 'only hindsight has endowed me with such a keen nose for nuance'. Their relationship is based on silence and a shared indifference to adults. (Silence is usually more communicative than speech.) But Gabriel always senses that Michael, that 'homunculus', is older because wiser. Gabriel has yet to discover evil. Like a pair of malevolent imps, they share a 'congenital coldness'. While Michael is left to run wild, Gabriel is forced to take lessons from Aunt Martha. She proves an utterly eccentric instructress, which pleases Gabriel, especially since in subjects like geography he learnt 'not its facts but its poetry'. She introduces him to a book, vaguely recalled as *The Something Twins*, and this fiction inspires Gabriel's misguided search for a long-lost sister called Rose. Now that he understands how and why this fantastic quest was plotted, he is frank about the value of what he refers to as 'necessary fantasy':

> There is no girl. There never was. I suppose I always knew that, in my heart. I believed in a sister in order not to believe in *him*, my cold mad brother. (172)

Michael may have tricked him, but Gabriel is glad to have

pursued the non-existent. Why? Because Michael, like the present, 'is unthinkable'. It was also a way of avoiding his darker self. Only fictions and idealisations offer protection and consolation. The psychological justification is transparent here, as when Gabriel remarks, 'I was not a cruel child, only a cold one, and I feared boredom above all else.' ('Accidie' was also Ben White's greatest fear.) Gabriel and Michael, the twin angels of hope and revenge, represent the principal conflict in *Birchwood*.

Gabriel sought escape from this boredom within his family by finding an alternative companionship based on a dream. This desire is temporarily satisfied in an encounter with the travelling circus: 'Prospero's Magic Circus' — which becomes his new and even stranger family. The circus is a collection of outlandish characters — the paternal figure of Silas and his 'companions', Angel and Sybil; the two men, Mario and Magnus; Rainbird, the scout and magician (who first appeared in *Long Lankin*); and ominously, two sets of twins, Ada and Ida, Justin and Juliette. This part of the novel, entitled 'Air and Angels', deals with the mystery of harmony between the physical and the spiritual, a theme echoed in the allusion to Donne's love-poem of the same name.[6] A whole range of literary and mythical allusions suggests a dramatic shift towards the exotic, and promises a fantastical and idealistic counterpoint to the oppressive atmosphere of 'The Book of the Dead'. The mythical names of the troupe, combined with the allusions to Donne, Shakespeare, Sheridan Le Fanu and even Nabokov,[7] serve to emphasise the blatancy of the fiction being pursued.

Gabriel's first problem with his new-found company is, predictably, consanguinity:

> I was confused. The names all slipped away from the faces, into a jumble. The tall slender woman with flame-red hair and agate eyes, Sybil it was, turned her face from the window and looked at me briefly, coldly. Still no one spoke, but some smiled. I felt excitement and

unease. It seemed to me that I was being made to undergo a test, or play in a game the rules of which I did not know. Silas put his hands in his pockets and chuckled again, and all at once I recognized the nature of the bond between them. Laughter! O wicked, mind you, and vicious perhaps, but laughter for all that. (107)

Everything about the circus family is deliberately unreal—the theatrical names, the exotic costumery and, above all, the suggestion of some diabolical 'bond' between them. Gabriel, of course, interprets the relationships wrongly, as the subtle allegiances within the group are obscured by appearances. Though Angel seems to be Silas's wife, Sybil is the mother of his twin-children, Justin and Juliette, the 'beautiful two-headed monster'. They are doubles in body and spirit, whom Marcus refers to as 'a single entity... called Justinette'. Silas's real lust, however, is reserved for the girl-twins, Ada and Ida, 'androgynous, identical, exquisite'. As if to complete this incestuous puzzle, the solitary child, Sophie, is the unintended result of a passing fancy between Mario and Ada, a couple alike in their 'incoherent rages, dark laughter', and 'careless cruelty'. The calculated mystery within this Gothic line-up is both spiritual and sexual, a riddle of harmony in which like and unlike seek out each other. The confusion of gender with the 'androgynous' twins, as with the hermaphroditic Molly Maguires, is Gabriel's most lasting fascination. Like the search for the fictional sister, it is a metaphor for the completion of the inadequate self.[8]

With the circus, Gabriel enjoys the exhilaration of imaginative release:

> Like our audiences, I also wanted to dream. I knew too that my quest, mocked and laughed at, was fantasy, but I clung to it fiercely, unwilling to betray myself, for if I could not be a knight errant I would not be anything. (118)

His romantic quest seems fulfilled in the character of Ida.

Unlike her twin, Ada, whose personality is savage and sadistic, Ida preserves a sense of child-like wonder, 'not innocence, but, on the contrary, a refusal to call ordinary the complex and exquisite ciphers among which her life so tenuously hovered'. Previous flirtations with girls had ended in physical farce, but Ida seems to embody the kind of spiritual beauty which makes the real world a scene of recurrent possibility. Looking back, Gabriel's image of Ida represents the kind of harmony forever threatened by a brute existence. His love for her, or rather his memory of that love, is the lyrical highpoint of *Birchwood*.

It is also, given the story's cruel logic, the signal for disaster. While picking blackberries with Gabriel, Ida is abducted and then beaten to death by the unannounced and inexplicable arrival of English soldiers. Recalling the tragedy, Gabriel expresses an acquired understanding of the power of evil—'Disaster waits for moments like this, biding its time.' It suggests an existence controlled by some diabolical sadist, sending the innocent on foolish journeys only to destroy them at the very moment of fulfilment.

Dreams turn, violently, into nightmares. The metaphor of twins represents a kind of existential schizophrenia, by which one aspect of self is confronted or pursued by another: Rose turns into Michael. The final confrontation between Gabriel and Michael suggests an acceptance of a terrible and fateful truth about the contradictions of the individual personality:

> Yes, he was my brother, my twin, I had always known it, but would not admit it, until now, when the admitting made me want to murder him. But the nine long months we had spent together in Martha's womb counted for something in the end. . . . His grin widened. He had not changed. His red hair was as violent as ever, his teeth as terrible. I might have been looking at my own reflection. (168–9)

Knowledge of this kind may solve the riddle of origin and identity, but it is little consolation after so much horror and death. Dramatically, this is a moment of terrifying self-recognition in which Gabriel must submit to his darker irrational self. This burdensome duality runs throughout the whole of Gabriel's recollection and creates the novel's alternating rhythm of hope destroyed by disaster, beauty by time, and self by anti-self. *Birchwood* is a romance which confronts everything that makes that ideal seem at once precious and impossible, vital and elusive.

As with so many romances, *Birchwood* depends on a version of childhood innocence. Gabriel writes, 'My childhood is gone for ever', and creates an elaborate fantasy that will console as well as explain. Although the pattern of the tale is one of inevitable, irrational violence, it also celebrates moments of wonder and ecstasy once felt and enjoyed. These moments alone justify the recreation of a nightmare and account for the novel's lyrical nostalgia. Gabriel pores over the past 'like an impotent casanova, his old love letters, sniffing the dusty scent of violets'. His love for Ida was one of those rare moments of faith: but even earlier ones are recalled which confirm his belief in the precarious survival of beauty, no matter how evil the world:

> Listen, listen, if I know my world, which is doubtful, but if I do, I know it is chaotic, mean and vicious, with laws cast in the wrong moulds, a fair conception gone awry, in short an awful place, and yet, and yet a place capable of glory in those rare moments when a little light breaks forth, and something is not explained, not forgiven, but merely illuminated. (33)

The nervous, hesitant and desperate tone of this conviction captures well the contradictory feel of *Birchwood*. Those 'rare moments' are usually unexpected intervals of imaginative and sensuous pleasure in which some small, redemptive sense of order and harmony is discovered. They are barely translatable moments of poetic inspiration, revealed in the most unpromising circumstances.

This is why the romance element in the novel is not just

Birchwood 41

about Ida or Rose. The two girls represent an important kind of spiritual and sensuous pleasure, but other moments are occasions of knowledge, of harmony perceived through the senses. A memorable example is when Gabriel and Michael first meet and try to find something to share. Gabriel shows Michael his favourite jigsaw 'of over two thousand tiny wafer-thin pieces'. In snatching this elaborate work from Gabriel, Michael lets it fall, and a horrified Gabriel is pained, not by 'the wasted work', but by 'the unavoidable recognition of the fragility of all that beauty'. To counter the disaster, and to show his power over Gabriel, Michael displays the art of juggling, using 'a chipped blue building block, a marble and a rubber ball'. Once in motion, the rhythm of this performance enthralls Gabriel:

> ... I found myself thinking of air and angels, of silence, of translucent planes of pale blue glass in space gliding through illusory, gleaming and perfect combinations. My puzzle seemed a paltry thing compared to this beauty, this, this *harmony*. (43)

Moments like this, when Gabriel achieves some sense of supernatural possibility through what at first seemed ordinary and dull, are the truly significant images of recollection. An almost abstract kind of knowledge is revealed through the seemingly insignificant, as if by magic. These epiphanies, as Geert Lernout calls them, 'really structure Gabriel's account'.[9]

The experience of the circus is, of course, a sustained sense of freedom of this kind, but usually these intimations of the divine or spiritual dimension of an otherwise diabolical existence are quickly overtaken by farce. As when Granda Godkin teaches the young Gabriel to ride a bicycle. The scene is hardly propitious. The boy is perched on a wreck of a bike, Granda puffing and wheezing alongside him, and a vicious dog attacking his heels. Gabriel is terrified:

> ... and then I felt a kind of *click*, I cannot describe it, and the bike was suddenly transformed into a fine delicate

> instrument as light as air. The taut spokes sang. I flew! That gentle rising against the evening air, that smooth flow onwards into the blue, it is as near as earthbound creatures ever come to flying. It did not last long, I jumped down awkwardly, landed on my crotch on the crossbar, and the back wheel ran over my foot. (58)

As the family name suggests, there is always a possibility of the divine in human affairs, but it is tragically rare and quickly dissipated by vulgar comedy. These epiphanies are always moments of silent intuition, beyond linguistic or intellectual account. The magical is revealed in the banal: the commonplace achieves a new significance. Perception always has this teasing, contradictory quality to it, as when Gabriel remarks, 'Violets and cowshit, my life has ever been thus.' This is why the quest for beauty and harmony is set during the Irish Famine. The exquisite can only be properly valued alongside the grotesque.

This sense of wonder, which appreciates the elusive beauty of the ordinary world, and which is forever threatened by madness and violence, is what Gabriel tries to recreate in his writing. Only the 'gentle Ida' seemed to personify such beauty and perception. *Birchwood* is a lament for the loss of such poetry at the hands of time and circumstance. As Seamus Deane puts it, Gabriel's story recreates 'a war of attrition between imagination and time'.[10]

Time, 'that word which gives me so much trouble', is central to Gabriel's sense of mystery and confusion. The purpose of his fictional version of the past is to defy, or at least conciliate, time. This partly explains why his chronology is often so confused. What matters to him, intensely, is to retrieve something of value from a past that resists accurate recollection, and so he invents, 'necessarily'. He writes in a form that will try to suggest an entirely subjective sense of understanding and knowledge. What he discovers only confirms his feeling of essential and preordained loneliness in the world. This sense of homelessness is expressed through an insight into the enviable order and pattern of time, especially the seasonal rhythm of nature. Like Stephen Dedalus in the opening chapters of *Ulysses*, Gabriel conducts his own physical experiments of vision and perception in order to understand the principles of reality and knowledge. Drinking with his circus family in a country pub, he plays a game of closing his eyes, then blinking rapidly, and suddenly 'it came to me with the clarity and beauty of a mathematical statement that all movement is composed of an infinity of minute stillnesses'. He calls this discovery an understanding of 'fixity within continuity'. Moving outside into the night air, the boy-astronomer contemplates the darkness and the stars, and senses yet again the paradoxical truth of the celestial order. In a typically self-conscious conclusion to this dream-like observation, he writes:

> And I saw something else, namely that this was how I lived, glancing every now and then out of darkness and catching sly time in the act, but such glimpses were rare and brief and of hardly any consequence, for time, time would go on anyway, without *my* vigilance. (128)

Such fine perception of subtle and delicate balance only deepens his sense of insignificance. For all his moments of revelatory joy, the world remains a mystery, its inhabitants strange. *Birchwood* ends on this note of alienation:

> Spring has come again, St Brigid's day, right on time. The harmony of the seasons mocks me. (175)

Even seasonal punctuality, however uncanny, contrasts with the chaotic mistiming of human activity, with its shocking catalogue of unexpected, inexplicable deaths and disasters.

This is a novel which thrives on its own contradictions. Gabriel insists that 'the past is incommunicable', yet recreates a version of it which tallies with that conviction. The novel's opening line, 'I am, therefore I think', by reversing the Cartesian principle of knowledge as intelligent command over experience, announces the futility of the enterprise in advance: the novel's concluding thought, 'whereof I cannot speak, thereof I must be silent', a direct quote from Wittgenstein, completes Gabriel's sense of resignation, by conceding the linguistic limitations of his narrative.[11] Language, unfortunately, chases an experience that cannot be captured.

Birchwood, with its twins, pairs, opposites and contradictions, is about the split personality of existence and perception. Oppressed by these tensions, Gabriel laments the fragility of beauty in a world 'capable of glory', but one also doomed to madness. His mother, Beatrice, 'with her pathetic faith in reason', is a victim of such madness. The 'Lawless' nature of human existence can be apprehended only through a dream-like imagery which captures its feel and quality. Gabriel offers nothing more than images which try to represent an experience too subtle for language. His father, Joseph, already knew the meaninglessness of his own life, which was why he tortured Beatrice and told his son that the whole domestic melodrama was about 'Nothing'.

Gabriel, in the third and final section of the novel, entitled 'Mercury', is supposed to be a messenger from the gods, a mediator between human and divine wisdom. The starving peasantry look upon him as a 'celestial messenger of hope'. But they are mistaken, since Gabriel has precious little to offer: the god of eloquence is struck dumb. Language seems too artificial a medium to evoke an experience so necessary but so difficult to recall. What he now remembers is meeting their suffering cries with contemptuous silence. Alone in the refuge of the ruined Big House, he writes that he does not even speak 'the language of this wild country'. He started writing about his childhood, so he believes, in order to give it a form and significance which, at the time, it seemed not to have. At the end of his memoir, he finds that it has little or no referential value. His fiction is no more than a suggestive but misleading duplicate of an experience that will always retain its own secrets—'Intimations abound, but they are felt only, and words fail to transfix them.'

So we are left with a fiction without pretensions to

knowledge, an imaginative pattern of events complete in itself, but no match for the ineffable nature of imaginative experience. Conversely, the copy, like Gabriel's jigsaw, sometimes improves on the reality it is supposed to represent. This is a most formal conclusion, elegiac and lyrical, caught between a real sense of imaginative relief and insight, and a contradictory sense of inevitable failure and loss.

Birchwood is a major advance on Banville's earlier fiction. Above all, it achieves an imaginative form perfectly suited to its theme. Less self-indulgent, more confident, it is a highly disciplined, yet playful, fable of the nature and meaning of memory and imagination. A novel that stresses the deceptive, illusory nature of its story has a special kind of credibility to sustain. In *Nightspawn*, this self-consciousness about the uselessness of writing became a medium for either playing intellectual games with a version of the superstitious reader, or an excuse for exercises in narrative obscurity. In *Birchwood*, by giving the story to Gabriel Godkin, a survivor of the events described, a more effective continuity based on a sympathetic character helps unify the novel. Rather than use Gabriel as a fictional stuntman, Banville uses him to convey a sense of personal and *felt* tragedy, of genuine grief and lasting pain.

In other words, the fiction about fiction is retained, but is now part of a convincing story about tragic illusion. The elaborate plot, and the central images of war and famine, give the story a dramatic setting crucial to the fictional intention of the novel. The mystery and confusion between identity, childhood, time and recollection are well served by the metaphoric intensity and inventiveness of the language, which finally accounts for so many of the original enigmas while simultaneously reinforcing the narrator's sense of wonder. Banville himself has commented on this paradoxical effect, saying, 'I like the end of *Birchwood*, where everything is wrapped up, and nothing is wrapped up.'[12] Whereas in *Nightspawn* this paradox is merely asserted, here it is achieved persuasively.

4

Doctor Copernicus

> What hath not man sought out and found,
> But his deare God? who yet his glorious law
> Embosomes in us, mellowing the ground
> With showres and frosts, with love & aw,
> So that we need not say, Where's this command?
> Poore man, thou searchest round
> To find out *death*, but missest *life* at hand.
> George Herbert, 'Vanitie'

IN a brief preface to *Doctor Copernicus* (1976), Banville acknowledges the help and inspiration of 'two beautiful, lucid and engaging books' in the composition of his novel, those by Arthur Koestler and Thomas Kuhn on the history of astronomy.[1] Both these studies offer eloquent accounts of scientific theory and speculation, accounts which provide a factual and historical structure for the novel. They also emphasise the importance of imaginative perception and the political context of such creativity. Readers familiar with Banville's work up to this point will recognise already the significance of these themes in his previous fictions. They will also recall Banville's fascination with the attraction between opposed forms of personality and perception. By turning towards the scientific career of Nicolas Copernicus, Banville's artistic imagination seeks out what modern man often takes to be the opposite of creative fiction. In this sense, *Doctor Copernicus* attempts a reconciliation between scientific and literary perception, just as classical astronomy sought to harmonise the earth and the heavens. A truly ambitious novel, it extends our appreciation of the role and power of fiction in man's attempt to understand his place in the order of nature. It is not just a literary version of a scientific career: it is also an assertion of the primacy of imagination in all forms of thought.

Perhaps we should start by trying to understand the attraction of the astronomer's personality and work. The historical evidence is not encouraging. Koestler says that 'Copernicus is perhaps the most colourless figure among those who, by merit or circumstance, shaped mankind's destiny.'[2] His chapter on Copernicus's only publication, *De Revolutionibus Orbium Coelestium*, is entitled, 'The Book that Nobody Read'.[3] As for the intrinsic value of *De Revolutionibus*, Kuhn remarks that its significance 'lies less in what it says itself than in what it caused others to say'.[4] Both historians agree that the Copernican revolution in astronomy is based on a strange paradox—it took place despite its author.

Like most of Banville's central characters, Copernicus is a writer. But this famous astronomer's relation to his solitary publication is based on a pattern of intrigue and betrayal which begins to suggest some of the dramatic and artistic possibilities that attract Banville. According to Koestler, Copernicus was terrified of publishing his work, largely because such a theory might not be verified by observation.[5] It might, he feared, turn out to be a complete fantasy. Secondly, in a time of political and religious upheaval, the appearance of a revolutionary theory might exacerbate social disorder and weaken respect for traditional authority. Yet the book was finally published, and nobody was scandalised. *De Revolutionibus* also seemed to reflect its author's ambiguous personality: as Kuhn points out, the treatise 'has a dual nature. It is at once ancient and modern, conservative and radical.'[6] Copernicus was a failure who, through the intervention of others, became a legend. His vision of the universe succeeded, not because his facts were consistent with observed reality, but because of their suggestive power. The sums were hopelessly wrong, but the idea was vital: words and signs may have failed him, yet the perception behind the disaster was inspired.

These are some of the historical aspects and motifs of Copernicus's career and theory which reappear in Banville's fictional study of the astronomer. Taken together, they offer an image of a paradoxical quest, a dream finally overtaken by the unpredictable and cruel forces of political reality.

The ambitiousness of *Doctor Copernicus* is partly fuelled by the Faustian myth that it employs.[7] Banville's story is about a specific form of intellectual ambition which tries to defy time and circumstance. Copernicus's early naivety and enthusiasm are soon replaced by a dehumanising obsession with a vision which denies the value and significance of the real world. Banville's version of the Faustian myth gives special place to a form of innocent perception, a recognition of concrete, earthly beauty which Copernicus ignores and, too late, regrets. It is a story about the terrible loneliness of such intellectual obsession and pride, but one which also strives for consoling redemptive knowledge.

The story of Copernicus's life and career, from childhood to death, is structured in four parts. The opening part, 'Orbitas Lumenque', deals with childhood and education in Prussia and Italy; the second part, 'Magister Ludi' (a nod at Hermann Hesse's novel?), is largely concerned with the traumatic relationship between Copernicus and his brother, Andreas; the third part, 'Cantus Mundi', is the only subjective narrative in the novel, and gives us a version of Copernicus by his student and disciple, Rheticus, who finally secured publication of *De Revolutionibus*; the final part, 'Magnum Miraculum', returns to the novel's third-person narrative, and follows Copernicus's mental and physical decline. This is the first time that Banville uses such a detached form of narrative, removed yet sympathetic, in order to dramatise the thoughts and feelings of his central character. Given the secretive and passive personality of Copernicus, it seems quite appropriate. The exceptional narrative by Rheticus, full of enthusiasm, bitterness and deception, is a familiar strategy in Banville's work. The relation between these narrative viewpoints has a dramatic significance to which I shall return.

The opening passages of *Doctor Copernicus* evoke the young

boy's innocent fascination with the relation between words and things:

> At first it had no name. It was the thing itself, the vivid thing. It was his friend . . .
> . . . Tree. That was its name. And also: the linden. They were nice words. He had known them a long time before he knew what they meant. They did not mean themselves, they were nothing in themselves, they meant the dancing singing thing outside. In wind, in silence, at night, in the changing air, it changed and yet was changelessly the tree, the linden tree. That was strange.[8]

Sensuous experience of the natural world comes before a language impatient to describe it. The passage, with its echo of the opening of Joyce's *A Portrait*, also makes concrete Gabriel Godkin's inverted dictum, 'I am, therefore I think.' The most curious aspect of this primitive contemplation is the supposed correspondence between words and what they represent:

> Everything had a name, but although every name was nothing without the thing named, the thing cared nothing for its name, had no need of a name, and was itself only. (13)

Language seems to have a dependent relation to what it signifies, feeding off something which exists separately and independently from it. Like Gabriel Godkin's jigsaw, it is a complex and ambiguous form of duplication. Banville begins with these innocent distinctions and definitions because he wants to dramatise a pure untarnished perception in which words are substituted for, but not confused with, things they represent. In the course of the novel, this distinction becomes tragically lost, until the astronomer mistakes a theory for the reality it was supposed to uncover and explain. Just as the writer works with a language which fondly imitates, but never matches, experience, so too does the astronomer devise a code of signs and symbols which he may foolishly substitute for a mystery beyond the grasp of such systematic reduction. Young Copernicus's sense of wonder is soon lost, and he 'learned to talk as others talked, full of conviction, unquestioningly'. In Banville's story, he spends the rest of his life in search of what he once knew.

But his quest for such obvious truths is not as simple or as preordained as I have perhaps suggested. Between innocent and mature forms of knowledge, Copernicus is not just the passive medium for a romantic parable of the genius of simplicity. The novel is never so sentimental or naive in its treatment of the process of knowledge, or of the relation between different modes of understanding. Copernicus's wisdom is acquired through coming to terms with everything he tries to deny. Before he attains such self-knowledge and acceptance, he must risk himself in the pursuit of absolute truth. One of the most convincing aspects of the novel is the way Banville dramatises the nature of this process of learning, a process that takes place as much in the real world of family and nation as in the lonely realm of the astronomer's mind. The drama of *Doctor Copernicus* lies in the attempt to reconcile the opposites.

As a young, enthusiastic and ambitious student of astronomy, Copernicus sees in science a possible order and harmony which will release him from the suffering and confusion of his present life:

> The firmament sang to him like a siren. Out there was unlike here, utterly. Nothing that he knew on earth could match the pristine purity he imagined in the heavens, and when he looked up into the limitless blue he saw beyond the uncertainty and the terror an intoxicating, marvellous grave gaiety. (32)

An important part of Banville's method of characterisation is to suggest this fateful compatibility between personality and pursuit. Astronomy, with its promise of order and harmony, is first an escape, an alternative to a wretched personal existence, and then a superior Platonic version of reality. It is an ambition that accommodates the young man's cold anxious personality. A certain kind of arrogance, however, the natural result of talent and enthusiasm, makes the young disciple dream of helping his masters to see the folly of inherited orthodoxies, based on Ptolemy, about the static nature of a fictional universe.[9] In a tense and embarrassing interview with Professor Brudzewski, an astronomer of the old school, the young Copernicus insists that science is so obsessed with schemes 'to save the phenomena', that all its work is redundant, merely a sophisticated language which fails to describe the actual nature of planetary motion:

> I believe not in names, but in things. I believe that the physical world is amenable to physical investigation, and if astronomers will do no more than sit in their cells counting upon their fingers then they are shirking their responsibility! (46)

In scenes such as these, personality provides an ironic counterpoint to theory. Copernicus's brave words, epitomised in the maxim that 'Knowledge ... must become perception', are intellectually sound and impressive, but his tact is abysmal. The interview ends with Copernicus exhausted and humiliated, warned by his professor that celestial mysteries may be named but never explained. Without knowing it, the young student has rejected the advice of his good angel, and will have to find out the truth in his own purgatory of confusion and suffering.

If Ptolemaic astronomy is no more than a fiction about the universe, an elaborate mathematical design with no interest in verification through observation, then Copernicus decides that his work must force a missing connection between the imaginary and the actual. Astronomy would no longer be an end in itself, but 'the knife' with which he would cut his way through the labyrinth of useless fictions about the world: it would become an instrument 'for verifying the real rather than merely postulating the possible'. The tragedy, both personal and intellectual, is that such a neat separation between means and ends proves impossible. The reason for Copernicus's failure lies with his denial of the inexpressible nature of mystery.

One of the great achievements of the novel is the way Banville traces this painful irony, as much in terms of the scientist's personal decline as in the growing realisation that the whole enterprise is doomed. Copernicus soon senses that the language of astronomy, whether words or mathematical symbols, indeed any language, cannot do justice to his perception. This humiliating discovery is the turning point of the novel. To his horror, Copernicus sees that his research takes on a life of its own, like his own personality, increasingly remote from the real world he was supposed to explain. What he writes now seems to him like 'gross ungainly travesties of the inexpressibly elegant concepts blazing in his brain'. The pitiful tragedy begins when Copernicus realises that he is trapped in the very dilemma he sought to banish:

> It was barbarism on a grand scale. Mathematical edifices of heart-rending frailty and delicacy were shattered at a stroke. He had thought that the working out of his theory would be nothing, mere hackwork: well, that was somewhat true, for there was hacking indeed, bloody butchery. He crouched at his desk by the light of a guttering candle, and suffered: it was a kind of slow internal bleeding. Only vaguely did he understand the nature of his plight. It was not that the theory itself was faulty, but somehow it was being contaminated in the working out. (105)

From the child who instinctively sensed the inadequacy of words in relation to the things they were supposed to represent, we are shown the intellectual adult come to a shocked realisation of the same truth. But the scale and enormity of the later perception make it tragic. Copernicus is mastered by a system he once believed was his willing servant.

Each of Banville's fictions up to this has contained some similar sense of the inadequacy of language, but here this unease becomes fully articulated in a mythical form which makes that sense of despair much more authoritative. In *Birchwood*, when Aunt Martha tries to teach young Gabriel the Latin for 'to love', the boy looks at his primer where 'the words lay dead in ranks, file beside file of slaughtered music'. But Copernicus's perception of this discrepancy amounts to a philosophical nightmare about the nature of knowledge, and his ability to account for reality. Long before the end of the novel, he realises that his work, directly contrary to ambition, is a self-contained fiction:

> He had believed it possible to say the truth; now he saw that all that could be said was the saying. His book was not about the world, but about itself. (128)

Copernicus is forced to accept that his theory is no more than what he calls 'an exalted naming'. Like all those ancient authorities he despised, his own work now joins a tradition of symbolic writing. As a humanist, he had sought to integrate the imaginary and the actual, but the connection did not take place. The heliocentric universe remains a revolutionary *idea*, the result of his creative inspiration and daring imagination. That, of course, is the basis of the Copernican 'revolution'. Banville always retains this fact, but wants to suggest the paradoxical character of the achievement. Copernicus is not just a Faustian stereotype: Banville's version of this tragedy adds the vital dimension of language as both means and obstacle to knowledge and perception.[10] The novel exposes the illusion of a certain kind of intellectual ambition which prides itself on the certainty and purity of its method: but it is also a sympathetic dramatisation of great imaginative need and yearning. The reasons for failure are not entirely due to the theory itself or to the language in which it is expressed. Alongside the monastic figure of the lonely canon, Banville has recreated a human society and a political world that are central to our interpretation of the story. The rhythm of this novel plays between Copernicus's celestial ambition and the gravitational pull of reality.

A major irony of *Doctor Copernicus* is that its hero, who devises a theory which suggests a limitless universe based on new planetary motions, tries desperately to deny the existence of comparable change in his own society. In this sense, he is both a prophet and a product of his age, engaged in work inspired by the humanist movement in Europe. Yet he is characterised throughout the novel as a man who will neither accept nor acknowledge the ordinary world he seeks to interpret:

> He believed in action, in the absolute necessity for action. Yet action horrified him, tending as it did inevitably to become violence. Nothing was stable: politics became war, law became slavery, life itself became death, sooner or later. Always the ritual collapsed in the face of the hideousness. The real world would not be gainsaid, being the true realm of action, but he must gainsay it, or despair. That was his problem. (38)

In his version of scientific hubris, Banville surrounds the astronomer with a pattern of friends, colleagues and disciples, all of whom, in different ways and with different motives, threaten to recall him to the everyday world of change and disorder.

The most important of these antagonists is his brother Andreas, whose personality and fate are in direct opposition to that of the cold secretive canon. Koestler refers to Andreas in terms that at once suggest why Banville adapted him to his narrative: he describes him as a 'rake', a 'mortally infected, contagious leper', who eventually died of syphilis.[11] Andreas is everything that his brother is not, and in the novel plays the role of Copernicus's haunted and guilty conscience. One of Banville's grotesques, Andreas is always there to confront his brother with the image of the world as hell. The astronomer's obsession with the heavens is parodied by his sibling's physical disintegration. As in *Birchwood*, Banville establishes a personal drama based on duality and opposition: Copernicus and Andreas represent a primitive duel between the angelic and the diabolical, as do Gabriel and Michael. The canon's philosophical sense of discrepancy between the ideal and the actual is reinforced by the tormented relationship with his ghastly brother. One finds consolation in the sky, the other in the brothel:

> There were for him two selves, separate and irreconcilable, the one a mind among the stars, the other a worthless fork of flesh planted firmly in earthly excrement. (37)

Copernicus's distinguishing feature is his frigidity.[12] Italy appals him with its reek of sexual decadence and political intrigue. His Prussian reserve is a mask worn by the intellectual to protect himself from all human contacts which threaten his choice of a solitary existence. Andreas's role is to show his brother a few home truths about the world.

The opposition between the two brothers is not just fictionalised at a realistic level, since each of them, but especially Andreas, has an allegorical dimension to his character in keeping with the novel's mythical structure. Copernicus watches in fear and helplessness his brother's disintegration and thinks of 'the terrible slow fall into the depths of a once glorious marvellously shining angel'. Andreas plays the role of a mocking Lucifer who enjoys tormenting his priestly brother. On one of his several visits to the canon's austere residence, the ghoulish Andreas taunts him:

> 'But tell me what *you* think of the world, brother', he mumbled. 'Do you think it is a worthy place? Are we

> incandescent angels inhabiting a heaven? Come now, say, what do you think of it?' (115)

Andreas's part is to voice an alternative vision of the world, fiercely sceptical in its honesty and despair, but never sentimental in its grief.

Much of Banville's fiction is based on this kind of dramatic personalised struggle between the forces of light and darkness. Put that way, however, the opposition is too abstract to do justice to the importance of sensuous detail in the author's creation of those extremes. This is particularly true of the grotesque element in his work. *Doctor Copernicus*, for example, documents physical suffering in all its horrific detail, so that the star-gazer's idealism is mocked by the reality he would prefer to ignore. He must witness what it is like to endure physical decay. In the presence of Andreas he can hardly ignore it:

> Now in the candlelight his face was horrible and horribly fascinating, worse even than it had seemed at first sight in the ill-lit porch, a ghastly ultimate thing, a mud mask set with eyes and emitting a frightful familiar voice. He was almost entirely bald above a knotted suppurating forehead. His upper lip was all eaten away on one side, so that his mouth was set lopsidedly in what was not a grin and yet not a snarl either. One of his ears was a mess of crumbled white meat, while the other was untouched, a pinkish shell that in its startling perfection appeared far more hideous than its ruined twin. The nose was pallid and swollen, unreal, dead already, as if there, at the ravaged nostrils, Death the Jester had marked the place where when his time came he would force an entry. (112)

This painstaking catalogue of horror is a powerful version of medieval corruption. With its reference to 'Death the Jester', it also conveys the grim irony of the *Totentanz*. Copernicus may represent the brave new world of the humanist adventurers, but Andreas is always there to remind him of an undeniable medieval underworld. This shocking contrast in imagery and personality is even suggested by the detail of Andreas's ears, the uncannily perfect one alongside 'its ruined twin', a residue of beauty within putrefaction. Flaunting his ugliness is Andreas's way of forcing his brother to accept mortality, and thereby that part of human affairs which no messianic idealism should discount.

For Andreas, suffering has become a means of knowledge which his brother is looking for, but in the wrong places.[13] The last chapter of the novel is a dialogue between the dying Copernicus and the ghost of Andreas, who announces himself as 'the angel of redemption'. In an elaborately surreal episode, Andreas reveals the kind of corrective wisdom which eluded his ambitious brother:

> With great courage and great effort you might have succeeded, in the only way it is possible to succeed, by disposing the commonplace, the names, in a beautiful and orderly pattern that would show, by its very beauty and order, the action in our poor world of the otherworldly truths. But you tried to discard the commonplace truths for the transcendent ideas, and so failed.
> I do not understand.
> But you do. We say only those things that we have the words to express: it is enough. (252)

Andreas's 'wisdom' would be mere sentimental naivety if his suffering was not such a convincing part of the novel. His idealism has been earned through pain and an understanding of the difference between language and knowledge, a respect for the limitations of language which leads to acceptance of inadequacy. He expresses passionate contempt for an ambition mediated through a language which confuses itself with what it tries to reveal. His is a kind of intellectual humility gained through a knowledge of evil and irrationality.

This resolution of the relationship between the two brothers lies beyond the drama of the astronomer's career, and is wholly invented by Banville in order to complete the intellectual and philosophical possibilities of the novel. The kind of redemptive insight offered by Andreas, which is based on an intense awareness of the significance of the actual is, paradoxically, quite a mystical conclusion to a story about the folly of abstraction and system. It recommends a reversion, through imagination, to a child-like perception of reality. Stylistically, it is a very polished coda to the relationship between the brothers, yet it is not the only, or the most satisfying, version of Copernicus's ambition. His relation to other characters offers us different narratives within the novel which tell us a different story, one without the mythical or mystical ambition of this particular relationship.

The third part of *Doctor Copernicus*, 'Cantus Mundi', is a dramatic and subjective narrative by Rheticus, the young and enthusiastic disciple of the great astronomer, professor of mathematics and astronomy at Wittenberg.[14] Rheticus served Copernicus for years, published his own preliminary treatise on the theory in 1540, the *Narratio Prima*, and then arranged for the first printed edition of *De Revolutionibus* in 1542: when the great work was finally published, it never once mentioned Rheticus. The devoted student got into trouble with the university authorities over his alleged homosexuality, and was transferred to Hungary where, in the last years of his life, he found his own disciple, Valentine Otho, who published Rheticus's mathematical researches. For Koestler, the story of Copernicus is markedly unsensational. The only drama in his career involves Rheticus, and it is documented as a tale of political intrigue and personal betrayal, themes that have always attracted Banville.

The novelist's interest in this disillusioned victim of his master's personality and ecclesiastical politics lies in the way his career mirrors that of his hero. Rheticus arrives in Copernicus's northern province of Ermland full of the same kind of babbling nervous enthusiasm which we have already noticed in his master's first interview. Writing many years later about his former self, Rheticus's account is a piece of revenge and self-vindication. Like Beckett's Malone, the voice is weary but defiant:

> I am at peace at last, after all the furious years. An old man now, yes, a forlorn and weary wanderer come to the end of the journey, I am past caring. But I don't forgive them! No! *The devil shit on the lot of you.* (171)

What follows is Banville's fictional version of an unacknowledged hero of astronomy. Rheticus's account is characterised by a splenetic outrage that his good faith could be treated with such contumely.

His vigorous, direct and often hysterical tale of working with Copernicus tries to lay bare the plot that exploited his labour and then dispatched him to the footnotes of history. His contribution to the novel dramatises the role of manipulative forces in what he mistakenly took to be an alliance devoted to pure knowledge. It is, we might say, a political as much as a personal version of lost innocence. He now believes that his greatest mistake was to think that science was free of the political influence of the Reformation. As a Protestant scholar from the heart of Reformation Germany, he did not realise that his relationship with Copernicus in Catholic Ermland was viewed by many, on both sides, as an unacceptable link. The humanist ideal did not reckon with the political designs and ambitions of a Machiavellian order of power.

His recollected evidence of betrayal is haunted by one consoling image of tenderness and love — that of Raphaël, a beautiful young boy who kept house for him. Rheticus is finally removed from his post because his superiors believe that he has corrupted an innocent. In this version of events, Raphaël becomes a function of the narrator's claim to innocence, and is recalled as the only source of joy in an otherwise degrading and corrupt past:

> ... that scene, I see it, and wonder that such a frail tender thing survived so long, to bring me comfort now,

and make me young again, here in this horrid place, Raphaël. I write down the name, slowly, say it softly aloud and hear aetherial echoes of seraphs singing. (212)

We see a familiar motif here. Just as Gabriel Godkin found, or invented, comfort through the romantic image of 'gentle Ida', so too does Rheticus defy his experience of evil and betrayal by preserving a dream of innocence. In both fictions, the nostalgic grief is made all the more poignant because of the dramatic and personal immediacy of the narrative form. Like Gabriel, Rheticus is making it up as he goes along. It is something of a predictable surprise, therefore, that we are told by Rheticus, near the end of his account, that Raphaël never actually existed. The fiction is a deceit. The reason he gives—'I had to find something, you see, some terrible tangible thing, to represent the great wrongs done me by Copernicus'—is understandable if pathetic. As with *Birchwood*, the tricks and illusions of memory are an important theme in this narrative. The empirical past must always be viewed, as Rheticus puts it, through the 'membrane of melancholy'. Personality and temperament seem to determine the tone and shape of his story: in medieval terms, the 'humour' of melancholy. Rheticus, like Ben White and Gabriel Godkin, is afflicted by depression, but 'worst of all is the heartache, the accidie'. A kind of dementia, born out of failure and isolation, informs Rheticus's obsessive narrative.

The historical reasons for Rheticus's outrage over the public presentation of *De Revolutionibus*, and his subsequent bitterness, seem uncannily appropriate to the fictional design of such a formalist writer as Banville. The historical structure of events concerning the long-awaited publication are retained by the novelist but he adds a dramatic picture of personal despair.

Although Rheticus originally supervised the early printing of the book, he was soon removed because of the charges of misconduct, and Andreas Osiander, a Lutheran theologian, saw the printing through to final publication.[15] When the book appeared, a horrified Rheticus and a bewildered Copernicus saw that Osiander had written a preface in which the entire theory was explained as a fiction, an account never intended as an explanation of actual planetary motion. The apologetic preface concluded:

> ... so far as hypotheses are concerned, let no one expect anything certain from astronomy, which cannot furnish it, lest he accept as the truth ideas conceived for another purpose ... and depart from this study a greater fool than when he entered it.[16]

A lifetime's work was now excused as a splendid, but inaccurate, fantasy, a 'post-modernist' fiction. Even the title of the work suffered a significant alteration, from *De Revolutionibus orbium mundi* to *orbium coelestium*, thereby severing any impression that the book was about reality.

Banville reinforces this irony by having Copernicus predict his own failure. The ageing astronomer, haunted by his brother's despair, confesses to a confused Rheticus the secret that has eluded him for so long, and that accounts for the colossal misunderstanding:

> You imagine that my book is a kind of mirror in which the real world is reflected; but you are mistaken, you must realize that. In order to build such a mirror, I should need to be able to perceive the world whole, in its entirety and in its essence. But our lives are lived in such a tiny, confined space, and in such disorder, that this perception is not possible. There is no contact, none worth mentioning, between the universe and the place in which we live. (219)

This submission, contracted partly from Andreas, is the beginning of Rheticus's madness. In Banville's post-modernist version, which relishes all forms of deception, Rheticus now confides that he was aware of the absurdity of the theory all along and kept his secret in the hope of climbing to fame on Copernicus's back. For Rheticus, the cruel farce is complete: the theory, though absurd, is publicly accepted, while his own vital role in the work results in oblivion. The anonymous canon is now famous, while the man who forced him into history is banished.

Rheticus is a victim, not just of his own superstitious veneration and academic cunning, but of a powerful and ruthless political order which is defined in terms of religious alliances.[17] One of the great dramas of the novel is the constant pressure of European politics upon the private careers of both men. The outcome of their research, as well as their shared despair, is deeply conditioned by their experience of the machinations of political and religious power. At one stage Rheticus had thought of himself and his master as 'angels, playing an endless, celestial game', but that fond belief was brutally overwhelmed by political expediency. Whatever the Church thought of *De Revolutionibus*, it would hardly have been diplomatic to have its preface signed by a Protestant homosexual. Copernicus tried, unsuccessfully, to keep the world of political and ecclesiastical intrigue at bay. He 'wanted no part in that raucous public world', yet it is forced upon him. Both men ignore or deny any connection between the private and the public worlds. Ultimately power insists on its supremacy over idealism.

The precarious existence of private ambition is always at the centre of the novel, and is mirrored in the political fate of Ermland, the would-be independent statelet surrounded by threatening empires. When his small country is the unexpected arena for major political ambitions, Copernicus is shocked by this barbaric intrusion into his academic hideaway. Once again Banville creates a character—Albrecht, grand master of the Teutonic Knights—who, in conversation with the gloomy astronomer, threatens his belief in the separability of the actual and the imaginary:

> Ah. The common people. But they have suffered always, and always will. It is in a way what they are for. You flinch. Herr Doctor, I am disappointed in you. The

common people?—pah. What are they to us? You and I, *mein Freund*, we are lords of the earth, the great ones, the major men, the makers of supreme fictions. (149)

This is an ominous moment for Copernicus, as Albrecht points out the similarity of their ambitions. For the cynical soldier, ordinary human suffering can be simply dismissed in the pursuit of a megalomaniac dream of conquest. Albrecht, like Andreas, is used by Banville to present a darker, sinister reflection of the astronomer's ambition. Like a pub-drunk, Albrecht assumes a familiarity that the scientist finds embarrassing, but, more importantly, quite just. Copernicus suffers from that familiar 'congenital coldness', a fear of intimacy and the flesh. In this novel Banville arranges a network of characters who warn Copernicus of the price of such a denial. As in *Birchwood*, the political background is there to show the fragility, sometimes the immorality, of escapism. Like Faustus, Copernicus learns and regrets this knowledge too late.

It is characteristic of Banville that such a personal tragedy should provoke an oppositional claim to an alternative faith that Andreas calls 'redemptive despair'. Both Andreas and Rheticus, for different reasons, reject Copernicus's nihilism. For Andreas, an understanding of reality comes from an acceptance of its madness. Only by submitting to the limits of knowledge, paradoxically, can any understanding of the world be attained. Andreas offers a faith based on humility, compassion and patience, a disposition towards ordinary experience that will open up a sense of the absolute. This is a form of mystical animism which strains to achieve a humane intensified alternative to the sterile vanities of intellect. The absolute is found in the concrete, and joy is reached through an acceptance of mortality. Contradiction is the real key.

Rheticus, more convincingly integrated into the resolution of the novel than Andreas, enjoys an unexpected consolation for his loss of faith. His rage is so personal that he insists that the Copernican theory which removes the earth from the centre of the universe is the direct result of its author's barren and perverse character. He believes that the heliocentric theory deliberately sets out to prove that 'the world turns upon chaos'. For Rheticus, Copernicus's book is the product of spite and evil:

> It destroyed my faith, in God and Man—but not in the Devil. Lucifer sits at the centre of that book, smiling a familiar cold grey smile. You were evil, Koppernigk, and you filled the world with despair. (231)

From this depth of anger and regret, Rheticus suddenly achieves, through a circumstance which gives him a final illusion of the prestige denied to him by Copernicus, a miraculous sense of transcendent hope and faith. An enthusiastic student, Otho, arrives to serve him in his research: as Rheticus says, 'The past comes back transfigured.'

This is the third and final version of the student–master bond, one through which Banville explores the relation between age and youth, hope and cynicism, future and past. The balance in that relation has favoured the power of disillusionment over faith. However, in a fiction which rejects the possibility of absolute forms of knowledge, hope assumes an earthly humanistic character. The master is reborn:

> I am Doctor Rheticus! I am a believer. Lift your head, then, strange new glorious creature, incandescent angel, and gaze upon the world. It is not diminished! Even in that he failed. The sky is blue, and shall be forever blue, and the earth shall blossom forever in spring, and this planet shall forever be the centre of all we know. I believe it, I think. *Vale*. (232)

Even the final, hesitant afterthought does not undermine the significance of this sudden revelation. It is left to Rheticus to express a new form of earthly wonder, inspired, ironically, by Copernican despair. Earth, dismissed from the heart of the universe, suddenly is brought into dramatic focus.

The heliocentric theory is the beginning of modern man's

sense of loneliness in the world. Like a second Fall, this new scientific fiction banishes humanity from the security of a static central presence in the world, to the reduced status of a small dependent sphere revolving in the cold wastes of the firmament. This is the real implication of Banville's cosmological drama.

The Copernican revolution is a falling from grace, the start of a modern sense of an impassable gulf between the spiritual and the material worlds. This loss is expressed through a passionate nostalgia for a sense of original unity of being. If restored, this might offer a clue to a new kind of redemption, the kind Copernicus imagined in Greece and Rome, 'when the world had known an almost divine unity of spirit and matter, of purpose and consequence'. Both Andreas and Rheticus articulate this alternative perception of man's desolation, and declare a new spiritual advantage in the loss of false certainties. Humanity, stripped of its original security, falls back on its own imaginative resources, and must cling to the beautiful and the concrete as the new forms of knowledge. It is the kind of wisdom, defined as poetic paradox, which Keats expresses in 'Ode on a Grecian Urn':

> Thou, silent form! dost tease us out of thought
> As doth eternity: Cold Pastoral!
> When old age shall this generation waste,
> Thou shalt remain, in midst of other woe
> Than ours, a friend to man, to whom thou say'st,
> 'Beauty is truth, truth beauty',—that is all
> Ye know on earth, and all ye need to know.[18]

This is not a religious form of consolation, but an aesthetic based on imaginative perception of the vital correspondence between nature and art.

A lyrical envy of nature, in its most enduring and concrete forms, concludes *Doctor Copernicus*. It is a poetic part of the myth of exile and alienation that informs Banville's fiction. *Nightspawn* and *Birchwood* ended with this same sense of diminishment in the face of nature's sublime indifference and remote beauty, and now Copernicus's final moments of consciousness recall a similar regret:

> ... Nicolas, straining to catch that melody, heard the voices of evening rising to meet him from without: the herdsman's call, the cries of children at play, the rumbling of the carts returning from market; and there were other voices too, of churchbells gravely tolling the hour, of dogs that barked afar, of the sea, of the earth itself, turning in its course, and of the wind, out of huge blue air, sighing in the leaves of the linden. All called and called to him, and called, calling him away. (254)

The gentle hypnotic rhythm of this concluding passage, its pastoral images of daily routine, capture a kind of emotional exhaustion after the distracted and obsessive pattern of his career. In a manner reminiscent of Gabriel Conroy's last sensations in Joyce's 'The Dead', it suggests a surrender to the rhythm of ordinary life. The final image of the novel recalls the opening one — the linden tree of childhood — as if to suggest, not just the endurance of this kind of concrete mystery, but a return to a perception denied and rejected for so long.[19]

Like much contemporary fiction, Banville's work is based on a contradictory self-consciousness about the relation between language and reality. The writer is forced to deal with a reality which cannot, or will not, be described. Writing about the futility of writing is a tricky enterprise. *Doctor Copernicus* is an adventurous version of that dilemma, all the more effective because its central character deals with symbols, not just the language of words. This version of the fiction-maker gives a unique and powerful generalising force to the myth of the inexpressible. The astronomer's greatness lies in his passionate determination and ability to construct a symbolic order: his tragedy and foolishness lie in his inability to recognise the deception of that order.

Banville's novel discovers an alternative security in the knowledge that language should not be confused with the mystery that it may evoke. By acknowledging the poverty of words, a renewed sense of their proper value is achieved. The poetic inspiration for this view is suggested in the epigraph to the novel, lines from Wallace Stevens's 'Notes toward a Supreme Fiction':

> You must become an ignorant man again
> And see the sun again with an ignorant eye
> And see it clearly in the idea of it.[20]

The opening section of the poem, from which the epigraph is taken, is about the need to trust imagination to do the work of naming the world, and not to allow perception to be deadened by the language of habit. The world comes first, as does the linden tree: what it is called remains of secondary and ambivalent value. Only by respecting and remembering this distinction will the burden of language become a revitalised means of knowledge.

A great new sense of fictional possibility has been opened up, and the balance between ideas and imagination, announced in *Doctor Copernicus*, will find its most satisfying harmony in the next part of the tetralogy—*Kepler*.

5

Kepler

> Yet the wanderer too doesn't bring from mountain to valley a handful of earth, of for all untellable earth, but only a word he has won, pure, the yellow and blue gentian. Are we, perhaps, *here* just for saying: House. Bridge, Fountain, Gate, Jug, Fruit tree, Window,—possibly: Pillar, Tower?... but for *saying*, remember, oh, for such saying as never the things themselves hoped so intensely to be.
>
> Rainer Maria Rilke, *Duino Elegies*

KEPLER (1981), continues the historical theme of *Doctor Copernicus*, the pioneering struggle of Renaissance science to open up a new vision of celestial and earthly order. Johannes Kepler, born in Swabia in south-west Germany in 1571, inherited the Copernican theory of a sun-centred universe. He was the first successor to give it a precise mathematical foundation based on painstaking observation, research that owed a great deal to Tycho Brahe, the Danish astronomer. Besides inventing the new science of dioptrics, the study of refraction, Kepler also formulated three important laws of modern physical astronomy.[1] Unlike Copernicus, Kepler was a prodigious writer and publisher, producing a series of major scientific works—*Mysterium Cosmographicum* (1597), *Astronomia Nova* (1610), *Dioptrice* (1612), *Harmonice Mundi* (1619), and a science-fiction fantasy, *Somnium*, published posthumously. The five chapters of Banville's novel are honorifically named after these works.

Kepler, like *Doctor Copernicus*, is a story about extraordinary ambition, but the contrast in personality between the eponymous heroes is the significant difference. A perfect contrast in spirit, but children of the same imaginative impulse, they are the adventurous twins of the new science. Whereas Copernicus, that 'mournful angel', was presented as a man who shunned any physical contact with family or the unpleasant side of earthly reality, Banville's Kepler is his most sympathetic character to date. Absolutely dedicated to his science and, like Copernicus, often seeing it as a defence against the disorder of religious and political realities, Kepler retains a compassion and innocence missing from his famous predecessor. If Copernicus succeeded despite himself, then the exact opposite applies to Kepler. The austere canon tried to keep reality at bay in order to contemplate the harmony of the spheres: his work, miraculously, survived. Banville's *Kepler* celebrates a character whose acceptance of ordinary reality yields the clue to his astronomical discovery and knowledge. *Doctor Copernicus* is about the tragedy of personality: *Kepler* is about the triumph of character.

As we would expect from Banville, *Kepler* is structured around a drama of anticlimax and revelation, rather than any strict chronology of a scientific career. The narrative pattern of the novel, like Kepler's famous discovery of orbit, is elliptical.[2] It begins, not with childhood, as in *Doctor Copernicus*, but with Kepler's first job as apprentice to the outlandish and eccentric figure of Tycho Brahe. This master–apprentice relationship, with its deceptive promise of inherited wisdom, is a version of the contest between arrogance and enthusiasm, experience and innocence, which is by now a familiar motif in Banville's fiction. In the opening scenes of *Kepler*, Banville arranges a pattern of ironic contrast which characterises the rest of his protagonist's life. Arriving at Brahe's castle of Benatek, outside Prague, the young Kepler's expectations are quickly and absurdly deflated. Greeted by a court dwarf instead of the host, surrounded by chaotic building-in-progress, and painfully aware of his outraged scolding wife, the anticlimax is yet another farcical version of the unexpected:

> Despite misgivings he had in his heart expected something large and lavish of Benatek, gold rooms and spontaneous applause, the attention of magnificent serious people, light and space and ease: not this grey,

these deformities, the clamour and confusion of other lives, this familiar—O familiar!—disorder.[3]

Revelation is the happier version of the shocking, but irony is the surer. Several of Kepler's flashes of momentous inspiration occur in the most outlandish and improbable circumstances, moments of exquisite joy and insight intensified by the chaotic and banal conditions of their birth. Yet Kepler's weary familiarity with being tricked by hope remains a basic conviction of his character.

The outstanding feature of that character is his refusal to submit to the temptation of despair. In theology he rejects absolutely the Calvinist doctrine of predestination: in science he retains faith in an imaginative order. Kepler's struggle is always with the unforeseeable. The most convincing part of Banville's story is when the dual nature of that mysterious intervention in human affairs is acknowledged: to equate the unexpected with the tragic is simply to define fate as a machine, rather than the instructive mystery Kepler believes it to be.

Much of our sympathy for the character of Kepler, especially for his endurance, comes from his personal innocence and social vulnerability. While waiting for the great Brahe to appear, Kepler, who comes from a poor background, is left watching the ordinary routine of the castle, a servant observing servants.[4] He is, as the narrator remarks, 'hopelessly of that class which notices the state of servants' feet'. As a picaresque hero, wandering all over Europe in search of peace and security in which to work and to raise his family, Kepler always remains outside the ranks of power and influence. Although working with Brahe and corresponding with the great Italian astronomer, Galileo, his physical existence is that of a scholarly tramp. This is another significant contrast with Copernicus, who thrived on monastic privacy and loathed everything adventurous or exotic. Felix, an Italian mercenary in Brahe's entourage, arouses only sympathy and envy in Kepler. Having nursed the soldier out of a fever caused by a terrible wound, Kepler is fascinated by this new bond between soldier and scholar, man of action and a dreamer:

> ... a kind of awful comradeship, by which he might gain entry to that world of action and intensity, that Italy of the spirit, of which this renegade was an envoy. Life, life, that was it! In the Italian he seemed to know at last, however vicariously, the splendid and exhilarating sordidness of real life. (69)

The childlike nature of this brilliant astronomer and mathematician, with his sense of wonder and adventure, makes Kepler such a sympathetic yet complex character. It is a quality that Koestler describes as a 'mystic's mature innocence'.[5]

Although Kepler as astronomer is the subject of the novel, his personal and domestic life are important for a full appreciation of his character. This relationship between the private and the public worlds is what provides the real drama in the novel. Copernicus's tragedy was the result of his determination to keep these two worlds utterly separate, being convinced that the everyday could teach him nothing. His brother Andreas tried to explain the personal and intellectual price to be paid for denying 'the splendid and exhilarating sordidness of real life'. As a counter-figure to Copernicus, Kepler is forever entangled with his family. The point of dramatising so fully this side of the scientist's career is not simply to romanticise Kepler as an 'ordinary man': on the contrary, it shows his special kind of imaginative empathy and perception, his sympathetic and symbolic way of reading the commonplace.

Portrayed as a shy husband, henpecked by a shrewish pitiful wife, Barbara, the great astronomer is a sorry spectacle. The domesticated scientist is an amusing, often farcical, element in the novel, but one with a serious purpose. Kepler works in the back-room on his theory of celestial harmony, while his wife is screaming in the kitchen about his lack of social ambition. Several children are born, most of them dying shortly after birth. Because of the religious and political wars in Germany and Austria, the family is forever on the move. This great astronomer, imperial mathematicus to Rudolph II, is entertained at court but never paid. His father-in-law worries about his daughter's financial situation, having married someone without a steady or a proper job. In the midst of all these domestic and public trials, Kepler has to deal with the legal authorities who have charged his mother with witchcraft. Even if he wanted to, Kepler cannot ignore the circumstantial world.

Banville pays detailed attention to the chaos and lunacy of Kepler's private life. At one level, it shows the impossibility of rising above the pressure of the mundane and the subjective, and recalls individual ambition to personal responsibility. But Banville's intention is not as moral as that might suggest. Kepler has indeed a lot to put up with, but so do those around him. Banville wants to represent a personalised version of chaos which is as instructive as the larger chaos in Kepler's struggle with the heavenly order. The domestic is, in many ways, an ironic counterpoint to the scholarly. At another level, its apparent irrelevance to ambition is entirely deceptive. Copernicus denied any significance to such details; Kepler never forgets them.

Kepler's appreciation of celestial harmony begins at home. The purpose of this irony is to intensify the contradictory and wondrous nature of a revelation that suddenly accepts the mysteriousness of the obvious and the obviousness of the mysterious. A central theme of *Kepler* is the ultimate simplicity of a kind of knowledge only achieved through labour of extraordinary complication and exhausting dedication. Ironically, it often seems to Kepler that he had already known what it took a lifetime to see. This ludicrous but uplifting insight is what connects the personal and the scientific in the story. Such a perception is finally revealed as innate—but it takes a lifetime of labour to recall. During that time, however, Kepler senses, on many occasions and through several personal relationships, the nature of the simple secret his intellectual pursuit obscures. Before looking at the scientific forms of revelation, we may note the pattern of personalised images of beauty and harmony in Kepler's turbulent domestic life which foreshadows his final vision.

When we first meet Kepler arriving at Benatek, he is accompanied by his wife Barbara and stepdaughter Regina. Inherited from his wife's previous marriage, Regina is his only consolation for this misalliance. As a figure of silent hypnotic beauty, she is a familiar image in Banville's fictional design, someone whose grace of character symbolises the kind of harmony usually absent from the world. Like Gabriel's Rose and Rheticus's Raphaël, she embodies an exquisite dream-like quality which corresponds to the astronomer's intellectual goal. In the middle of one of many domestic arguments, Regina's magical presence is observed by Kepler:

> Regina came in, effecting a small but palpable adjustment in the atmosphere. She shut the big oak door behind her with elaborate care, as if she were assembling part of the wall. The world was built on too large a scale for her. Johannes could sympathize. (20)

This silent observation, based on imaginative empathy for such delicacy of motion, all the more precious for its contrast with the drudgery of the row, is a characteristic effect of the whole novel. Regina is one of those symbolic characters who represent a mute form of innocent and natural harmony which Kepler will eventually discover in the divine universe. She is evidence, in earthly form, of the magical in human affairs.

Kepler's love for his stepdaughter (relationships in Banville are rarely conventional) endures for most of his life. At the height of his fame, but still struggling with the laws of planetary motion, optics and physical astronomy, Kepler continues to be fascinated by her oracular presence:

> Why was it, he wondered, that her candid gaze so

> pleased him always; how did she manage to make it seem a signal of support and understanding? She was like a marvellous and enigmatic work of art, which he was content to stand and contemplate with a dreamy smile, careless of the artist's intentions. To try to tell her what he felt would be as superfluous as talking to a picture. (99)

Characters like Regina represent an aesthetic ideal, a non-intellectual, lyrical image of innate beauty. She has read her father's work, but offers no opinion on it. Her role, of course, is quite different from that of colleague or commentator: she is a premonitory presence who offers a clue to what her scholarly father seeks through intellect.

Having seen this kind of platonic relationship before, in *Birchwood* and *Doctor Copernicus*, it is not surprising, however disappointing, that such love turns sour. Regina marries, and Kepler feels abandoned by the only spiritual love in his life. To make his disappointment all the more bitter, her new husband supervises letters to Kepler, hounding him for settlement of dowry and inheritance money, completing the sense of degradation. There is an important fictional difference between Regina and the corresponding figures of Rose and Raphaël: she is not, as they are, figments of the imagination. She is, for a while, a living consolation whose reality amid chaos makes her seem all the more unreal.

Other members of Kepler's family reveal a similar kind of primitive innocence. This is especially true of Heinrich, Kepler's younger brother, a hulking epileptic, a former soldier, now living like a big child with his sorceress mother. Kepler's fascination with Heinrich is based on the same sense of contrast that he felt between himself and Felix, the mercenary. One of life's inarticulate victims, but full of awe and curiosity for his famous brother, Heinrich's ignorance and experience intrigue Kepler:

> But he had been to the wars. What unimaginable

spectacles of plunder and rape had those bland brown eyes witnessed in their time? From such wonderings Kepler's mind delicately averted itself. He had peculiar need of *this* Heinrich, a forty-year-old child, eager and unlovely, and always hugely amused by a world he had never quite learned how to manage. (93-4)

Like Regina, Heinrich *feels* the world rather than knows it. Kepler has yet to experience this sensation, although he can empathise with it. Images of innocence, mute and intuitive, play an important part in the development of his perception and knowledge. These images are reminders of a different imaginative outlook which Kepler always respects, but which comes to him at the end of his life by a most circuitous route.

Banville's attraction to Kepler lies in the relation between character and achievement. Now that we have looked at the nature of that character and its private dimension, we should turn to the science that transformed character into genius. Banville's novel accepts the outline of Kepler's scientific career, especially the arduous discovery of new laws of planetary motion. His fictional interest in the historical Kepler lies more with the actual process of discovery than with the scientific facts of that process.

Kepler's first 'discovery' — that the universe is based on five perfect geometric forms — was quite false, as fictional as anything in Copernicus. Kepler announced this principle of symmetry in his first book, *Mysterium Cosmographicum*, which is also the title of the novel's first chapter.[6] It is not difficult to see Banville's fascination with the fictional character of this scientific proposition. Kepler, while teaching at a school in Graz, is wondering why there are only six planets, and why the distances between them seem so fixed:

> On that ordinary morning in July came the answering angel. He was in class. The day was warm and bright. A fly buzzed in the tall window, a rhomb of sunlight lay at his feet. His students, stunned with boredom, gazed

over his head out of glazed eyes. He was demonstrating a theorem out of Euclid—afterwards, try as he might, he could not remember which—and had prepared on the blackboard an equilateral triangle. He took up the big wooden compass, and immediately, as it always contrived to do, the monstrous thing bit him. With his wounded thumb in his mouth he turned to the easel and began to trace two circles, one within the triangle touching it on three sides, the second circumscribed and intersecting the vertices. He stepped back, into that box of dusty sunlight, and blinked, and suddenly something, his heart perhaps, dropped and bounced, like an athlete performing a miraculous feat upon a trampoline, and he thought, with rapturous inconsequence: I shall live forever. (30)

The angel of revelation always arrives unexpectedly and unannounced into the most prosaic of situations. Kepler's discovery here is intuitive, accidental and false, but it is the richest error in his scientific career.[7] Looking at the figure on the blackboard, he believes that geometry is the key to the design of the physical universe. There are six planets, the logic argues, because there are only five perfect solids known to science, and the solids 'fit' perfectly and harmoniously between those planets, revealing the distances between them. Kepler's mystical faith in geometrical form and the supernatural significance of numbers is part of his neoplatonic and neopythagorean inheritance.[8]

The idea of geometrical symmetry as the divine plan of a harmonious celestial order is pleasing as a theory, but Kepler cannot prove it mathematically. This *a priori* discovery forces him, through a lifetime's work of observation and calculation, to achieve his famous laws of physical astronomy. For Banville, Kepler's revelations show the crucial role of imaginative faith, even if it is initially no more than fiction. In this instance, the fiction of a geometric universe is especially significant to the novel, as it suggests a simple form of harmony at the heart of the universe. Fiction, it turns out, may be the surest road to reality. This, on Banville's part, is an artistic compliment from one formalist to another.

The path from fiction to fact is the real imaginative miracle of the novel. It is a dramatisation of insight by one of Koestler's great 'sleepwalkers', a discovery based as much on accident as design, on vision as on intellect. The story of Kepler's career demonstrates, above all, the primary truths of imagination and the intellect's slow return to what imagination originally reveals. Kepler's first law, announced in his second book, *Astronomia Nova*, declares that the planets move, not in circles, but in elliptical orbits. Because of his misleading obsession with perfect shapes, he took years to discover what he knew was already there. This intellectual search for mathematical confirmation of the ellipse is the primary motif of the novel's design, an enigma to which the narrative keeps returning. The secret first occurs to Kepler in the opening lines of the story, while he sleeps and dreams:

> Johannes Kepler, asleep in his ruff, has dreamed the solution to the cosmic mystery. He holds it cupped in his mind as in his hands he would a precious something of unearthly frailty and splendour. O do not wake! But he will. Mistress Barbara, with a grain of grim satisfaction, shook him by his ill-shod foot, and at once the fabulous egg burst, leaving only a bit of glair and a few coordinates of broken shell.
>
> And 0.00429. (9)

The theatrical manner of the narrator, with his Prospero-like evocation of mystery, lifts the curtain on a childlike genius. For the reader, the final number, set apart as a significant afterthought, stands alone without explanation. What does it mean? The reader, like Kepler, will have to wait. The mysterious number is given to us at the opening to suggest a knowledge that has yet to be consciously understood.

As an apprentice to Tycho Brahe, Kepler is deliberately assigned to the observation of Mars, a planet with the most eccentric orbit of all. This piece of spite on Brahe's part, eventually leads to Kepler's greatest discoveries; but he immediately lays a wager that he will solve the riddle of Mars in seven days. Seven years later, he makes the final breakthrough. In a letter to a friend, in the *Harmonice Mundi* section of the novel, Kepler details the excruciating process of his discovery that the equation 0.00429, a figure in his mind all those years, turned out to be the formula for an ellipse:

> There is a final act to this comedy. Having tried to construct the orbit by using the equation I had just discovered, I made an error in geometry, and failed again. In despair, I threw out the formula, in order to try a new hypothesis, namely, that the orbit might be an ellipse. When I had constructed such a figure, by means of geometry, I saw of course that the two methods produced the same result, and that my equation was, in fact, *the mathematical expression of an ellipse*. Imagine, Doctor, my amazement, joy & embarrassment. I had been staring at the solution, without recognizing it! Now I was able to express the thing as a law, simple, elegant, and true: *The planets move in ellipses with the sun at one focus.* (148)

Not only does Kepler, to his mortified amusement, discover what he knew, but he wonders at the workings of the human mind and its strange teasing progress. The moral of such an irony is not, of course, that the scientific labour was a waste of time. On the contrary, however Sisyphean such a labour might seem, Kepler emerges as a heroic indomitable figure. Intellect is simply a slow affair compared with imagination: but sometimes it is the only path back to a kind of understanding obscured by science. When Kepler triumphantly concludes that the law was 'simple, elegant, and true', we are reminded of Regina's character. The imaginative intellect of Kepler has discovered, or rather confirmed, the underlying simplicity of the celestial harmonies. The details of his theory of the five perfect solids were wrong: but the purity and the symbolism of the idea were true. In that same letter to his friend, Kepler writes, 'Thus we do progress, my dear Doctor, blunderingly, in a dream, like wise but undeveloped children!' Kepler's greatness, in contrast to Copernicus's, lies in this kind of humility. For him, the greatest discovery of all is his understanding of imaginative perception as the link between human and heavenly order.

All this is to characterise Kepler as a neoplatonist, an astronomer who insists on the symbolic relation between the actual and the ideal, the material and the spiritual. The clearest and most eloquent expression of his philosophy comes in the fourth chapter of the novel, *Harmonice Mundi*. Based on a circular pattern of twenty letters from Kepler to ten recipients, composed of family and colleagues, it is the only chapter in which Kepler speaks directly, free from the ironic sympathy of the narrator. The letters begin in 1605, progress up to 1612, and then return to their starting point. This elliptical pattern is a playful device by Banville to both imitate the key geometric image of the novel and to illustrate the pattern of original enlightenment. Just to heighten the symbolism of this pattern, the letters begin and end with the season of suffering and transfiguration—Ash Wednesday and Easter. It is a chapter whose rhythm, form and structure are worthy of the great astronomer himself, who declares in one of the letters, 'It is ever thus with me: in the beginning is the shape!' Progress, according to this pattern, is an inexorable form of recollection.

Throughout these letters Kepler explains his belief that the universe is based on geometric forms placed there by God, hence the perfection of the spheres. To understand God's creation requires an understanding of these forms. This knowledge, Kepler insists, is latent in every person, but only revealed through imaginative perception. His work has discovered a divine harmony which was already inscribed in the mind and soul:

> In this I take issue strenuously with Aristotle, who holds

> that the mind is a *tabula rasa* upon which sense perceptions write. This is wrong, wrong. The mind learns all mathematical ideas & figures out of itself; by empirical signs it only remembers what it knows already. Mathematical ideas are the essence of the soul. . . . the mind determines how the eye must be, and therefore the eye is so, because the mind is so, and not vice versa. Geometry was not received through the eyes: it was already there inside. (146)

The tribute to God is also a tribute to a human perception capable of seeing His reflection. Man, in this special sense, is the centre of Kepler's universe, the real *magnum miraculum*. Kepler's joy is the result of this *human* discovery, his recognition of the divine with the earthly. All his work has led him back to a sense of simple, intuitive and original harmony.

Banville's stylistic expression of these discoveries is not always in such an exalted tone. Kepler's belief in the miracle of perception, as well as the beauty of that which is perceived, is eventually conveyed in the rather formal mode of scholarly correspondence. But the actual moments of revelation which are afterwards formulated as laws, are a typical mixture of the sublime and the ridiculous. We may recall Kepler's amazement at the significance of the forms he casually chalked on the classroom blackboard, all the while nursing his injured thumb. Later, he hits upon the principle of uniform velocity for these elliptical orbits while retching into a street-drain after carousing with whores in a tavern. (We may recall Godkin's vision of the stars and the principle of 'fixity within continuity', after tumbling out of the country pub.) Only once, in his sudden insight into a third law concerning the mathematical relation between a planet's period and its distance, does Banville omit any ironic form of deflation. This time, inspiration comes in truly celestial shape:

> When the solution came, it came, as always, through a back door of the mind, hesitating shyly, an announcing

angel dazed by the immensity of its journey. One morning in the middle of May, while Europe was buckling on its sword, he felt the wing-tip touch him, and heard the mild voice say *I am here*. (176)

The imagery of angelic inspiration is a common feature of Banville's fiction, as we saw with *Birchwood* and *Doctor Copernicus*. The difference in *Kepler* is that its beatific character has no diabolical counterpart. Kepler, unlike Copernicus, is the great synthesiser. The aptly named *Harmonice Mundi*, Kepler's final vision of world harmony, is the work which brings together the human and the divine, the imaginative and the rational.

The story of Kepler's achievement is one of exalted serendipity. So much is discovered that was not looked for, especially this new appreciation of the shaping power of the imagination. In his early days, Kepler, like Copernicus, had thought of science as a realm of abstraction and order that would defend him against the violence and sectarianism of European politics and a chaotic personal life. But, like the pattern of the *Harmonice Mundi* chapter, his achievement brings him back to an original innocence which illuminates the ordinary spontaneous world he would rather have denied.

Celebration of the ordinary and visible reality of God's design is a recurrent and organising motif in the novel, at first only an impression, but finally a spiritual revelation. Throughout Kepler's story, there are intimations of this secret harmony and beauty, always alternating with scientific struggle and political danger. This pattern of renewed vision based on recollected images is seen, for example, in the episode where Kepler and his wife, at the height of a row over payment from Brahe, leave the castle and appeal to Baron Hoffmann for help. They are met with the same kind of patrician arrogance as before. Distracted by these humiliations, Kepler suddenly hears music through the window and walks over to look into the garden:

> The rain shower had passed, and the garden brimmed with light. Clasping his hands behind him and swaying gently on heel and toe he gazed out at the poplars and the dazzled pond, the drenched clouds of flowers, that jigsaw of lawn trying to reassemble itself between the stone balusters of a balcony. How innocent, how inanely lovely, the surface of the world! The mystery of simple things assailed him. (62)

This lyric image, in its careful arrangement of sensuous and orderly detail, suggests a delicacy and sensitivity in the perceiver as well as in what is being perceived. Banville's way of animating certain scenes, especially here with the image of the lawn 'trying to reassemble itself' like a jigsaw, always emphasises the vitality of Kepler's way of looking at the world. The scene represents a coming together of the poetic and scientific visions. Much later on in his researches, while labouring with an astronomical chart for the Emperor Rudolph, and hating his bondage to power of this kind, the image of that garden scene floats back:

> The demented dreamer in him rebelled. He remembered that vision he had glimpsed in Baron Hoffmann's garden, and was again assailed by the mysteriousness of the commonplace. *Give this world's praise to the angel!* He had only the vaguest notion of what he meant. (84–5)

It may still be no more than an intimation for Kepler, but for the reader, perhaps, the significance is clearer. The celestial voice which Kepler hears, a quotation from the visionary poet, Rainer Maria Rilke, urges him to celebrate the sensuous world, to see it anew in the light of his heavenly experience.[9] Banville is trying to capture a visionary experience of the ordinary, whereby the tangible world assumes a new significance. With this renewed sense of the beauty and magic of the natural world comes an appreciation of man's proper human scale. Kepler realises that harmony is not so much an objective set of facts about an uninhabited realm of the universe, but a faculty of ecstatic perception. He now recalls a scene from his childhood, long forgotten, which confirms this new sense of wonder. He remembers his innocent fascination at watching a snail crawl up a window-pane:

> Pressed in a lavish embrace upon the pane, the creature gave up its frilled grey-green underparts to his gaze, while the head strained away from the glass, moving blindly from side to side, the horns weaving as if feeling out enormous forms in air. But what had held Johannes was its method of crawling. He would have expected some sort of awful convulsions, but instead there was a series of uniform small smooth waves flowing endlessly upward along its length, like a visible heartbeat. The economy, the heedless beauty of it, baffled him. (98)

This mesmeric image of delicate patient ascent suggests Kepler's own somnambulant career. Such a miniature form of struggle and effort, in a place which shows the beauty and the absurdity of such determination, gives the onlooker an insight into man's humble place in the vastness of creation. At the end of the novel, sick and delirious, Kepler dreams of the same image of small but wondrous survival—'Turn up a flat stone and there it is, myriad and profligate! Such a dream I had . . . *Es war doch so schön*'.[10] The stargazer, whose story begins and ends with a dream, has rediscovered his earthly sphere.

Kepler is one of Banville's most romantic figures, someone Koestler describes as 'the most reckless and erratic spiritual adventurer of the scientific revolution'.[11] His attractiveness lies in a childlike sense of fascination which he never loses, which is paradoxically restored by science. He is also a man of courage and determination. However much preoccupied by the stars, Kepler has to fight to survive in a Europe dominated by political and religious intrigue. Without this background of persecution and cruelty, which does not spare Kepler and his family, the novel could only assert intellectual achievement. 'Pure' science does not exist in the novel: it emerges only after doing battle with time and circumstance. Like Godkin, Kepler is a miraculous survivor.

Kepler's story is marked by constant exile. As a Lutheran, but a famed astronomer, he is only just tolerated in Catholic Austria; in Lutheran Germany, he is suspected of Calvinism. The looming Thirty Years' War manipulates his fate as surely as the astrologer's stars. Like Copernicus, he detests politics: unlike Copernicus, he never takes sides:

> In the matter of faith he was stubborn. He could not fully agree with any party, Catholic, Lutheran or Calvinist, and so was taken for an enemy by all three. (161)

Banished finally from Austria, then excommunicated by the Lutheran church, Kepler's only consolation is his work and what remains of his family. Religious politics repeatedly intrude on his life, setting up a constant tension between the private and the public sphere. While working for the Emperor on the Rudolphine Tables, he is summoned home for the arraignment of his mother as a witch. In an extraordinary scene in which the inquisitors display the instruments of torture to encourage a confession, Kepler notices his mother's proud but dangerous indifference to the drama around her. After such a hard life, the stubbornness of the old woman evokes her son's 'rueful admiration'. Later, his wife Barbara contracts typhus, which the Austrian troops had brought with them into Prague. For the first time, Kepler appreciates what she had to endure and pays tribute to her in a letter to Regina. His favourite son, Friedrich, aged six, dies of smallpox, '. . . a fair child, a hyacinth of the morning in the first days of spring, our hope, our joy'. One of his favourite friends, Wincklemann, a Jewish lens-grinder, has gone missing, another victim of inquisitorial enthusiasm. Kepler's personal life is a series of cruel disasters, yet his dream of harmony and beauty becomes all the more necessary.

Kepler's heroic quality comes from his refusal to despair. Overwhelmed by personal grief, cheated and betrayed by political and religious authorities, he finds consolation in a picture of artistic stoicism based on faith:

> The vision of the harmony of the world is always before me, calling me on. God will not abandon me. I shall survive. I keep with me a copy of that engraving by the great Dürer of Nuremberg, which is called Knight with Death & the Devil, an image of stoic grandeur & fortitude from which I derive much solace: for this is how one must live, facing into the future, indifferent to terrors and yet undeceived by foolish hopes.[12] (128)

This is very much like the image of his mother before the inquisition. Kepler's faith in himself is calm yet eloquent, humanistic yet deeply religious. Like all romantics, he defies the world to beat him down. His idealism seems authenticated by the horrors that it has to endure and overcome.

The important role of imagination in Kepler's character is formally underlined, as we have seen, by the dreams that introduce and conclude the novel. A pleasing historical coincidence between Banville's characterisation and his hero's private writings is found in the title of the novel's final chapter, *Somnium*, a science-fiction fantasy which Kepler composed at intervals in his career.[13] It is about a future visit to the moon in which Kepler tries to fictionalise some of his theories about force and gravity. In the final episode of Banville's novel, Kepler looks back on his writings:

> None of his books had given him such peculiar pleasure as this one. It was as if some old strain of longing and love were at last being freed. The story of the boy Duracotus, and his mother Fiolxhilda the witch, and the strange sad stunted creatures of the moon, filled him with quiet inner laughter, at himself, at his science, at the mild foolishness of everything. (183)

The astronomer is secretly a novelist. His fabulous fiction, in which the man is transformed into a boy, and accompanied by his strange mother, is Kepler's most satisfying book because it harmonises the dream of childhood with the knowledge of adulthood. By 'childhood' Banville seems to suggest not so much the actual state itself, but a mode of vital perception. Kepler smiles at 'the mild foolishness of everything', because he realises the ultimate absurdity of trying to explain mystery. His imaginative side laughs at his rational side to see how long it took to recognise what was simply there. He also smiles because now he remembers that so many examples of this truth were already revealed to him in different forms. His old friend, Wincklemann, for example, possessed this mystical knowledge:

> What was it the Jew said? Everything is told us, but nothing explained. Yes. We must take it all on trust. That's the secret. How simple! He smiled. It was not a mere book that was thus thrown away, but the foundation of a life's work. It seemed not to matter. (185)

Kepler has found a strange paradoxical consolation: loss is transformed into a new certainty, and ignorance suddenly seems full of renewed significance.

Put abstractly, the novel is about an epistemological tug-of-war between two kinds of knowledge, the imaginative and the intellectual, the primitive and the scientific. Kepler harmonises old and new forms of understanding, opening up original modes of perception based on ancient faith in a harmonious universe. Though dismissing the use of astrology for political ends, he believes in the heavenly influence of the stars upon human character: he also believes passionately in the new science of physical astronomy which promises knowledge based on reason and observation. Ultimately, his knowledge is part of the humanistic movement, as much a contribution to mankind's expanded perception as a triumph of self-understanding.

Although Kepler is attracted towards two very different kinds of knowledge, he is never stranded between them. Whereas Copernicus is represented as a scientist without faith or love, Kepler is a most sociable hero. This quality gives the second novel in the tetralogy a very different effect. In *Doctor Copernicus*, Banville had to represent a largely negative character and outlook: in *Kepler*, he can celebrate a human as well as a scientific achievement, and relate both to a poetic form of seeing the world. Because of its central character, *Kepler* is a simpler, less tortured, more lyrical novel, whose playful sense of harmony and design is directly inspired by its subject. Copernicus and Kepler, we might say, represent the most dynamic version of opposites in Banville's fiction so far. Like Michael and Gabriel in *Birchwood*, these twin-figures of imagination complement each other's vision. One stands for despair, the other for hope: together, they complete Banville's story of the creative struggle between science and poetry.

6
The Newton Letter

> History is nothing more than the belief in the senses, the belief in falsehood.
>
> Nietzsche, *Twilight of the Idols*

AFTER the epic scale of *Doctor Copernicus* and *Kepler*, the third part of Banville's tetralogy has a very different, but not unfamiliar, character. Subtitled 'An Interlude', *The Newton Letter* (1982) is a novella that plays a new contemporary version of the astronomical theme.[1] In several ways, it represents a relaxation of the historical structure of the original design, and a return to earlier features of Banville's fiction. The progress of the tetralogy, however, still matches the scientific advance of the intellectual revolution begun by Copernicus and culminating in the work of Isaac Newton (1642–1727), whose discoveries in the fields of gravity and optics were strongly based on Kepler's achievement. With Newton, the humanistic alliance between imagination and reason is concluded.

The 'Letter' in the novella's title is based on a biographical incident that Banville uses and reinterprets in order to complete his gallery of 'those high cold heroes who renounced the world and human happiness to pursue the big game of the intellect'. In September 1693, after months of silence, Newton had sent to his friend, the philosopher, John Locke, a paranoid letter containing wild accusations of betrayal and conspiracy.[2] A reconciliation followed, but Newton henceforth abandoned science. Biographical arguments and interpretations over his nervous collapse and withdrawal are crystallised by Banville's second 'Letter', a borrowing from Hugo Von Hofmannsthal's fictional 'Ein Brief'.[3] This second letter is used to explain the first, and suggests that the crisis has been caused by a dramatic imaginative change, a revelation consistent in expression with the alternative visions of Copernicus and Kepler. As with the first two astronomers, Banville has reshaped the historical character of his protagonist in order to complete a dramatic conflict between scientific knowledge and imaginative perception. Many of the facts are already there, awaiting selection: the novelist replaces them in a new fictional context in order to intensify the personal drama behind speculative accounts of experience.

The novella takes the form of an autobiographical memoir addressed to Clio, the muse of history. Told by an anonymous biographer of Newton, it relates the short and painful events of his stay in County Wexford while trying to write his book. A personal crisis forces him, like Newton, to abandon the research. Everything is transformed by this personal trauma: biography becomes autobiography, detached scholarship becomes an anguished letter. By another trick of time and imagination, the biographer's fate mirrors exactly that of his seventeenth-century subject. The title of the novella becomes an ambiguous message about the powerful influence of the imagined past on the present.

Looking back on more innocent times, the narrator-scholar recalls his arrival in Ferns, County Wexford, where he sought peace and privacy in order to write his study of Newton. He rents accommodation from the Lawless family, Charlotte, Ottilie and Edward, owners of a run-down Big House. Delighted by the calm and grace of these apparently typical Protestant landowners, who have style if not money, he looks forward to a rural idyll while researching his *magnum opus*. This plan is confused by his growing intimacy with the family. A child, Michael, also appears in the house. The narrator remembers being baffled by the precise relationship between the four residents. Despite a lustful affair with Ottilie, he secretly yearns for Charlotte. Edward turns out to be a former nurseryman on the estate, not a brother, while Michael belongs to none of them, having been adopted. Other mortifying discoveries follow: the Lawlesses are, in fact, Catholic, and Edward's strangeness is the result of a terminal disease, not of shyness. No longer trusting his assumptions, frustrated in love, bewildered and saddened by the mysteries of this strange household where appearances always trick him out of confidence and belief, the biographer decides to abandon both his research and the country. Instead of returning to Cambridge, he finds a new post in Finland, a place more congenial to his chastened heart. Ottilie writes to tell him of her unexpected pregnancy. Hearing this news, his narrative ends on a mixture of hope and dread for the future. It is a confessional tale of intellectual failure and imaginative hope.

In form and style, *The Newton Letter* breaks with the narrative pattern of the tetralogy and recalls the more personalised account by Gabriel Godkin in *Birchwood*. In quite a daring synthesis, Banville has produced a Big House version of the scientific mind. The Lawless family name signals this adaptation of an Irish setting and genre to the scientific theme. The plot reveals other familiar correspondences between the two fictions—the enigma of actual family relations as opposed to the narrator's original presumptions; the presence of Michael, 'unbending silent, inviolably private'; and a final sense of the inadequacy of the text itself. On a thematic level, as Geert Lernout argues, *The Newton Letter* 'answers the questions formulated in *Birchwood*'.[4]

Despite these correspondences with *Birchwood* and their altered function within the tetralogy, the novella has a narrator who is a new figure in Banville's fiction—the academic. As a disillusioned scholar, he tries to recall the reasons for a loss of faith in what he calls 'the primacy of text'. This gives his recollections an ironic tension and self-conscious unease, a manner that mocks his earlier personality:

> I'm confused. I feel ridiculous and melodramatic, and comically exposed. I have shinned up to this high perch

and can't see how to get down, and of the spectators below, some are embarrassed and the rest are about to start laughing. (10)

After seven years of writing his biography of Newton, the narrator no longer believes in the value or meaning of his interpretation. In an uncanny way, he is re-enacting the story of his own book. This is why there are two alternating tales in the novella: the one set in contemporary Ireland, the other a biographical recreation of Newton's crisis of belief. Wiser now, the narrator realises that the original separation of thought and experience that led to Newton's breakdown is precisely his own problem. Like the great scientist, he experiences the revolt of language against his ego, and is left with a childlike sense of wonder at the mystery of ordinary experience. Before reaching that state, however, he singles out the scholar-type for self-mockery, because of its deadening use of language. Receiving a copy of another biography of Newton, by an enthusiastic colleague named Popov, the narrator contemplates the stereotype:

> I met him once, an awful little man with ferret eyes and a greasy suit. Reminded me of an embalmer. Which, come to think of it, is apt. I like his disclaimer: *Before the phenomenon of Isaac Newton, the historian, like Freud when he came to contemplate Leonardo, can only shake his head and retire with as much good grace as he can muster.* Then out came the syringe and the formalin. That is what I was doing too, embalming old N.'s big corpse, only I *did* have the grace to pop off before the deathshead grin was properly fixed. (29)

This scathing caricature of the scholar, contemptuous and witty, captures the narrator's sense of guilt and relief. Glad to be deceived no longer by the foolishness of a certain kind of intellectualism, he is now writing a very different sort of story which will try to recover the personal experience that was responsible for his disillusionment. This time, he will have the advantage of a sceptical self-knowledge.

Apart from the digressions on Newton and the biography, most of the story is about tragic flirtations with Ottilie and Charlotte. The experience of that summer in Ferns is described as a series of shocks and revelations which were always unpredictable and usually shameful. The academic's early confidence of thought and action is repeatedly undermined by people and relationships whose appearance is totally misleading. Nothing, it now seems, was ever entirely innocent. Formerly, the scholar thought of himself as the hero of the drama: now he realises that he was only the dunce. Writing about it now, his retrospective story tries to suggest the strangeness of that past, an unreal quality best described through literary analogies of a contrived art:

> Then I would see Charlotte herself, in wellingtons and an old cardigan, hauling out a bucket of feed to the henhouse. Next comes Ottilie, in a sleepy trance, with the child by the hand. He is off to school. He carries his satchel like a hunchback's hump. Edward is last, I am at work before I spy him about his mysterious business. It all has the air of a pastoral mime, with the shepherd's wife and the shepherd, and Cupid and the maid, and, scribbling within a crystal cave, myself, a haggard-eyed Damon. (20)

The past is a literary fiction filled with familiar conventional types acting out prescribed parts. At one point the narrator recalls rushing along the lawn with Ottilie after the child has had an accident—'We must have looked like an illustration from a Victorian novelette, marching forward across the swallow-swept lawn.' Ottilie's parents, killed in a car accident, are described as 'a kind of Scott and Zelda, beautiful and doomed'. All these fictive analogies create a dream-like quality in the narrator's account of the past, and suggest the crucial and misleading role of expectation in shaping and defining experience. He now realises that he invented a version of the Lawlesses which was a second-rate fiction. All the time thinking he knew what was going on, he now knows that his patronising image of the family deluded him into a series of interpretations that only served to expose his innocence. Pastoral and intellectual fictions were part of a secret design in which he unwittingly played a prescribed role. He now admits that 'Even the unbroken fine summer weather was a part of the plot.' Ordinary experience has taught him the lesson of his life, and humbled his conceit.

The narrator recalls being assailed by unanswerable questions about the exact relationship between the Lawlesses, especially the question of the child who, like a malevolent Cupid in this demented romance, never says a word. At first he thought Michael was Ottilie's child, then Charlotte's. But Edward? Did he seduce the young Ottilie? Why, then, is he sleeping with Charlotte? Only now does the narrator appreciate Edward's loneliness, his 'sense of oneness with all poor dumb things'. It turns out that most of his suspicions about the incestuous family are melodramatic and groundless. He also discovers that Edward used to write poetry, but, like the scholar and the scientist, has abandoned the work.

Loneliness and boredom are also the sources of Ottilie's affair with the biographer. Initially very passionate, the relationship starts to cool when the narrator realises that he has confused the two women, an entity he calls 'Charlottilie', and that he secretly longs for Charlotte.[5] No longer working on his book, he becomes fascinated by 'this spawning of multiple selves' and hypnotised by the 'daily minutiae' of the little drama in the enclosed world of Ferns. One part of him continues the physical affair with Ottilie, while the other fantasises about Charlotte. The sexual flirtation soon palls, and his treatment of Ottilie becomes cruel and cold. His longing for Charlotte is really a form of vanity, since he sees himself rescuing her, as a gallant intruder, from an alcoholic Edward. After a while, assisted by his lurid imagination, he begins to sense a latent madness in the family:

> They were altered, the way someone you have known all your life will be altered after appearing, all menace and maniacal laughter, in a half-remembered dream. Up to now they had been each a separate entity. I hadn't thought of them as husband and wife, mother, son, niece, aunt—aunt!—but now suddenly they were a family, a closed, mysterious organism. (67)

As in previous fictions, Banville tries to convey a primitive and sinister sense of mystery behind conventional facades. Following a crisis, the everyday and the familiar, when contemplated so intensely, become frighteningly significant. It is as if nature has been spying on the biographer all the time. This is the eerie feeling expressed at the opening of the novella when he recalls his trip past Killiney on the train down to Wexford. Details and images of the landscape then seemed quite innocent, but now he feels that they colluded in his self-deception: '. . . such remembered scraps seem to me abounding in significance. They are at once commonplace and unique, like clues at the scene of a crime.' This analogy captures perfectly the bizarre quality of his experience and later revelation: the observer becomes the observed. His world is alive with signs and meanings, an animate significance undreamt of by intellect.

The fictional conceit played out in *The Newton Letter* is one whereby the biographer's mental crisis one summer in Wexford, has already been scripted by Newton's identical breakdown in the summer of 1693 at Cambridge. Without realising it, the historian was looking at a prefiguration of his own fate. This strange coincidence of roles, whereby a historical fiction reappears in a new and most unlikely setting, chills the biographer's heart because it suggests a subtlety of design and purpose he had never imagined. This is the point at which the alternating narratives of the story coincide, and the scholar sees himself reflected in Newton's plight. Earlier detachment from his research is now replaced by a feeling that the history book has become a weird kind of disguised autobiography.

This is the revelation of Newton's second fictional letter to which the biographer keeps returning. His own commentary, alive with a growing sense of something familiar, reflects on the details of Newton's crisis:

> But then suddenly he is talking about the excursions he makes nowadays along the banks of the Cam, and of his encounters, not with the great men of the college, but with tradesmen, the sellers and the makers of things. (59)

Newton tries to explain to Locke that the ordinary sensuous world seems to be addressing him, but in a language without words. After the scientific exploration of absolutes of time, space and motion, he suddenly feels that relative human truths are more mysterious. Once he senses that the common world of experience contains this cryptic significance, Newton writes:

> *My dear Doctor, expect no more philosophy from my pen. The language in which I might be able not only to write but to think is neither Latin nor English, but a language none of whose words is known to me; a language in which commonplace things speak to me; and wherein I may one day have to justify myself before an unknown judge.* Then comes that cold, that brave, that almost carven signature: *Newton.* (59)

This literary echo from Hofmannsthal,[6] grafted onto his historical fiction about Newton's crisis, completes Banville's tale about the scientist, while suggesting an epistemological reason for the biographer's change of heart. Through Hofmannsthal's lines, the novella suddenly assumes a self-reflexive character, a rhetorical hesitancy, which is at the heart of the post-modernist dilemma. The crisis, not surprisingly, is about language. Once it suffers from such profound suspicion, expression is never quite the same again. This is, of course, Banville's favourite territory, in which that sense of dislocation and separation between words and experience struggles for fictional harmony. Artistically, if this mystery is to remain mysterious, then the nature of the revelation that follows the disillusionment with language must remain rhetorical and assertive. A new faith, even if it concedes the inadequacy of words, or the superiority of silence, must be proclaimed.

The biographer, finally exiled in the cold North, and now corresponding with Ottilie, comes to enjoy some kind of compensatory hope after failure in County Wexford. Simply to fail and despair is never the pattern of Banville's fiction. Disillusionment, especially with language, always reveals an alternative, usually richer, way of seeing and writing. When the biographer hears from Ottilie that she is pregnant with his child, he experiences a unique sense of elation mixed with fear. The idea of a child gives him a feeling of inexpressible wonder at human accident and design. For the first time, he feels creative and certain of immortality, (like Kepler), summing it up in Rilke's line, 'Supernumerous existence wells up in my heart.'[7] Such lyrical joy, we are made to feel, has been earned out of confusion and deception. It is all the more authentic in a context where such desperate hope is always mindful of the probability of destruction:

> Yet I'm wary. Shall I have to go off again, leaving my research, my book and everything else unfinished? Shall I awake in a few months, in a few years, broken and deceived, in the midst of new ruins? (92)

Hope, qualified by fearful experience, and terror, softened by memories of joy, hold between them the ambivalent experience typical of Banville's characters. Like Kepler, the persona in *The Newton Letter* is too maimed by experience to be naive, but is also too imaginative to despair.

In Newton, Banville found and exploited a pattern of experience, from intellectual achievement to a chastened innocence, which is a major theme of the tetralogy so far. It is announced in the novella's famous epigraph about playing as a boy on the seashore, 'whilst the great ocean of truth lay all undiscovered before me'.[8] The story of Copernicus ended with the linden tree of his childhood; Kepler's last work was a fantasy about a boy and his mother travelling to the moon. Newton's anecdote reinforces this motif of innocence after experience. Even the biographer, in his foolishness, 'felt briefly like a child, pressing his face against the cold unyielding pane of adult knowingness'. This is a pattern of experience and perception based on a paradoxical inversion of development. Even though most of Banville's writers question the value of their intellectual sanity or achievement, the stories should not be construed as anti-intellectual or in any way scornful of scientific ambition and curiosity. Only such a mind, allied to imaginative character, can fully appreciate the limits of intellect so intensely. As with the mystic monks of early Christianity, only by isolation in the sterile loneliness of the desert can the beauty of human creation be discovered.

As an 'Interlude', *The Newton Letter* is a leisurely stylish episode in the demanding scale of the tetralogy. Although certain forms and themes will be familiar, the novelty lies in its economy, its sustained mood of hypnotised fascination with images of the past, and, we should not forget, its sly humour.

7
Mefisto

> Writing may not really be able to give voice to utter desolation, to the nullity of life, to those moments when it is simply a void, privation and horror. The mere fact of writing in some way fills that void, gives it form, makes the horror of it communicable and therefore, even if minimally, triumphs over it.
>
> Claudio Magris, *Danube*

MEFISTO (1986), presents us with a strange resolution to Banville's tetralogy. A reader who has followed this extended narrative of the scientific imagination, which began a decade beforehand with *Doctor Copernicus*, will inevitably have developed expectations of style and theme. This is especially true of the historical dimension of the series, including *The Newton Letter*, despite the novella's disarming subtitle of 'An Interlude'. So far, much of the authority and fascination of these fictions lie with the recreation of famed, historical genius. However, as Banville himself has remarked, such a framework was invented to serve his own themes, and not simply to give us a historical fiction obedient to fact.[1]

As a coda to the tetralogy, *Mefisto* retains many familiar motifs and dramatises them, not in the world of Renaissance humanism but, as in *The Newton Letter*, in modern Ireland. This time, Banville has chosen not to centre his fiction on a name associated with creative genius. Rather, *Mefisto* is a demonic and mythological conclusion to a series dominated by the Faustian legend.[2] Finally, after three tales of frustrated ambition and paradoxical achievement, it is the turn of that malevolent character behind the pitiful hero to assert his power over human enterprise.

The novel takes the form of a Proustian recollection by a single narrator, Gabriel Swan. In many ways his story recalls *Birchwood* rather than the series which it is supposed to conclude.[3] Swan's story, a phantasmagoric blend of memory and fantasy, is about his survival. It tells of his strange childhood as a mathematical prodigy who escapes from home and rural boredom into a world of bizarre and freakish companions, then experiences appalling suffering and isolation, clings desperately to a dream of love and order, and is finally reduced to writing what he calls this 'black book', in order to reach some understanding of his wreckage. The only obvious features of the novel which confirm its place in the tetralogy are the boy's mathematical prowess, a gift that is never fully explored, and the legendary title-character who eventually appears under the different, perverse name of Felix. Whatever Banville's intention, *Mefisto* retains a symbolic rather than a substantial connection with its 'scientific' predecessors. As a tortured memoir of childhood, it echoes the form of *Birchwood*; as a bizarre adventure, it resembles the fictional contrivances of *Nightspawn*. No matter how we classify or categorise it (always a tempting exercise with such a parodic and allusive writer as Banville), *Mefisto* is an eclectic blend of the familiar and the original.

The motif of twins or a twinned identity reappears as the central image of the novel.[4] Whether as contrast or opposition, this idea of a split or dualistic personality, forever at war with itself, is also at the heart of the Faustian legend. Banville uses this traditional drama of the sundered personality to dramatise a distinctively modern sense of isolation and alienation. In *Mefisto* he develops the motif to suggest a fateful, inherited and deterministic pattern of chance and design. Swan's memoir begins, as did Godkin's, with his foetal existence:

> I don't know when it was that I first heard of the existence, if that's the word, of my dead brother. From the start I knew I was the survivor of some small catastrophe, the shock-waves were still reverberating faintly inside me ... The perils we had missed were many. We might have been siamese. One of us might

have exsanguinated into the other's circulation. Or we might simply have strangled one another. All this we escaped, and surfaced at last, gasping. I came first. My brother was a poor second. Spent swimmer, he drowned in air.[5]

This gestation and birth, a contradiction between design and chance, cleverly provides Swan's tale with an opening myth of original and fundamental mystery based on hazard. Existence then becomes an extension of that opening trauma, a life characterised by inexplicable and precarious survival. Swan's entire narrative preserves this distinctive sense of shock and fascination. His quest is not, like that of Godkin, for a lost half, but for the significance of the numerical order behind such a random and schizoid existence.

The motif of twins also accounts for the story's obsession with 'freaks of nature', a phrase that captures both the original marvel and Banville's method of characterisation. At school, the young Swan is mesmerised by another pair of twins, especially by 'the thought of being able to escape effortlessly, as if by magic, into another name, another self . . . .' Feeling part of this exotic brotherhood explains his preoccupation with, and subsequent gift for, numbers:

> I remember a toy abacus that I treasured for years, with multicoloured wooden beads, and a wooden frame, and little carved feet for it to stand on. My party piece was to add up large numbers instantly in my head, frowning, a hand to my brow, my eyes downcast. It was not the manipulation of things that pleased me, the mere facility, but the sense of order I felt, of harmony, of symmetry and completeness. (19)

How or why the phenomenon of twins should lead to such an interest is a less convincing part of Gabriel's character than his extraordinary receptivity towards the grotesque and the odd. This attraction is a predetermined curiosity towards wondrous creatures who allow him to forget his ordinary existence and to indulge his rare imagination.

Mefisto 101

Gabriel's narrative is in two complementary parts, 'Marionettes' and 'Angels', the first based on innocence and wonder, the second on pain and horror. In similar but less stereotyped fashion than *Birchwood*, it recalls a familiar kind of anguished family surrounding a stubbornly silent child. Mathematical fantasies are the child's only escape from an embittered mother and an indifferent father. Bored by school and home, Gabriel accidentally encounters the weird new inhabitants of the local Big House in Ashburn, an exotic trio whose influence on him is fatal. The first of these is Mr Kasperl, a large, sinister, ruminative Faust, who surveys the local countryside for some shady mining company. Like so many of Banville's characters, he is strikingly bisexual in appearance, with an 'odd womanly walk, at once ponderous and mincing'. With Kasperl is a young woman called Sophie, a deaf and dumb beauty whose silent grace and playfulness contrast pointedly with her restless unnerving companion. The third member of this outlandish group is Felix, the actual 'Mefisto' of the novel, and one of its most convincing characters. When first recalled, Felix resembles something between a cartoon-villain and a tramp:

> He was thin, with a narrow foxy face and high cheekbones and a long, tapering jaw. His skin was pale as paper, his hair a vivid red. He wore a shabby pinstriped suit, that had been tailored for someone more robust than he, and a grimy white shirt without a collar. (35–6)

Felix is the diabolical medium of the story, a mocking and sadistic tempter who persuades young Gabriel to join the bizarre company in the cavernous interior of Ashburn House. In contrast to his fictional cousin, Godkin, this Gabriel escapes *into* the decaying world of the Big House, an omen of the disaster that awaits him.

For the rest of 'Marionettes', the narrative is more concerned with recollected perceptions and impressions of these characters than with events and episodes which develop the story. Kasperl, who never says a word, spends all his time writing out elaborate mathematical equations which are part of his mining project. Gabriel is enthralled by this fellow sorceror—'But his was a grandmaster game, and I was a novice. Such intricacy, such elegance!' Sophie seems to him as mysterious as the hieroglyphics in Kasperl's book:

> She communicated in an airy, insubstantial language consisting not of words but moving forms, transparent, yet precise and sharp, like glass shapes in air. (55)

Her silence seems a gift rather than a defect, a choice that intensifies her awareness and responsiveness. Felix is always a malicious but witty presence around this childlike couple, every-ready with ironic literary captions for their silent hypnotic relationship. He dubs them 'Hansel and Gretel', refers to Sophie as Keats's 'still unravished bride of quietness', and to Gabriel, ominously, as 'bird-boy'. Like a fiendish jester, he is forever playing some contrived role, speaking mostly through literary quotation and pun. His names for Gabriel include Malvolio, Icarus, Caliban, Castor, Philomen and Melmoth, names that both define and anticipate Gabriel's search for a new identity. Names in *Mefisto*, as in all of Banville's previous novels, have a deliberately contrived, mythical or allusive significance in order to emphasise a character's frank sense of unreality and artificiality. Gabriel's recognition of this sense of fictive manipulation occurs in a scene when Sophie arranges a game of toy-marionettes for the boy, giving each of the figurines a familiar face in miniature. Gabriel contemplates the life-like puppets:

> I thought of the marionettes, twitching on their strings, striving to be human, their glazed grins, the way they held out their arms, stiffly, imploringly. Such eagerness, such longing. I understood them, I, poor Pinocchio, counting and capering, trying to be real. (118)

Only uncanny metaphors like these speechless toys correspond to Gabriel's sense of unreality. This same sense of fictional recognition is expressed in his love of fairy-tales in which '... there was something dismayingly familiar... the mad logic, the discontinuities, the random cruelty of fate'. That description captures perfectly the design and ambition of *Mefisto* itself.

Gabriel comes to realise that Felix has pimped Sophie and himself for Kasperl's sensual and intellectual needs. The mining project, however, meets with disaster when the pits explode without warning. The townspeople turn against the strange outsiders and Felix announces his abrupt departure, while assuring Gabriel that they will meet again. The boy, now abandoned by his new sinister family, wanders back to Ashburn House to contemplate the marionettes once more. Suddenly, an inferno overwhelms the house and Gabriel remembers falling through the flames. Whether the fire was accidental or the result of local revenge is left ambiguous.

The second section of the novel, 'Angels', recalls Gabriel's horrific return from immolation to a barely human existence. In the opening pages of this nightmarish episode, he details the pain of his new life as a physical freak:

> Scorched hands, scorched back, shins charred to the bone. Bald, of course. And my face. My face. A wad of livid dough, blotched and bubbled, with clown's nose, no chin, two watery little eyes peering out in disbelief. (125)

Gabriel has become a monstrous marionette himself, at the mercy of the 'ministering angels' in the hospital, human and medical. He survives through pain-killers, which he calls collectively 'Lamia', the deceptive serpent-woman of Keats's mythological poem.[6] If 'Marionettes' represents an innocent, vulnerable way of seeing the world, then 'Angels' reveals that same world in permanent darkness and pain. In grotesque form, Gabriel is now reborn. In his first existence, he was a freak of biological chance; now he is a deformed casualty of human circumstance. There is a nightmarish pattern to his lonely existence, sadistic and unpredictable. One day he wanders into the maternity ward and studies the new-born babes, 'prune-faced mites in their plastic coats', and recognises himself. Once he has recovered enough mobility to walk, he is turned out into the unknown and unexperienced world of the metropolis. Like the babes, he has just been released into reality but, unlike them, has already suffered its madness.

The pattern of events and the nature of characters in 'Angels' are very similar to those in 'Marionettes'. The only significant difference is that now the city becomes a surrealistic hell of an underworld in which Gabriel finds new, and old, friends.

He first meets the ubiquitous Felix, who recognises Gabriel instantly, remarking breezily, 'I never forget a face.' He then introduces the boy into a company almost identical to that of Ashburn House. A wizened old professor, Kosok, a reincarnation of Faust, is in charge of a scheme which illegally uses a fabulous computer to investigate a project that is never explained. Felix, as before, 'procures' Gabriel to assist Kosok in this mathematical labyrinth. They are joined by Adele, a sorrowful junkie (who, we are told much later, is Kosok's daughter), and a motley assortment of types drawn from the seedy, outrageous world of drug-trafficking and industrial espionage. Gabriel offers two valuable gifts to this underworld—his unlimited supply of drugs from the hospital and his passion for mathematical enigma.

The plot of this section, like Gabriel's fairy-tales, is random in the extreme. As in a fun-fair ghost-tunnel, freakish and lurid figures simply pop up, disappear, never to be seen again. The most coherent part of the narrative concerns Gabriel's new painful sensitivity to the world about him, where 'everything was new and yet unaccountably familiar'. He has a farcical affair with Adele, who offers him physical intimacy in exchange for drugs: the search for mathematical harmonies is as frustrating as the yearning for love. Kosok's computer fails to yield up any of its abstract secrets, notwithstanding Gabriel's ingenuity. Months go by with Gabriel silently drifting between the unobtainable and the inexplicable. The climax of this fruitless activity occurs one evening when, in a bar full of addicts to whom he ministers, Gabriel decides to step outside the claustrophobic frenzy in order to reflect on his situation:

> Then suddenly I was outside in the cold black glossy night, under an amazement of stars. I could smell the pines, and hear the wind rushing in their branches. My head swam. Something surged within me, yearning outwards into the darkness. And all at once I saw again clearly the secret I had lost sight of for so long, that chaos is nothing but an infinite number of ordered things. Wind, those stars, that water falling on stones, all the shifting, ramshackle world could be solved. (183)

This revelation, identical in spirit and situation to that of Godkin in the 'Air and Angels' section of *Birchwood*, is the clearest link between *Mefisto* and the predominant theme of the tetralogy. Like Copernicus, Kepler and Newton, he realises that abstraction has prevented him from seeing the obvious. Such a realisation must admit, in hindsight, that this perception is based on a simple but deceptive paradox—'the more I knew, the less I seemed to understand'. Even Kosok, driven to his wit's end by the inscrutable machine, screams at his superiors in exasperation, 'You want certainty, order, all that? Then invent it!' Like his illustrious fictional predecessors, Gabriel can finally see the crucial difference between system and purpose. Numbers, he realises, are a method, and not the end, of knowledge. In a familiar expression of resignation, he now sees that 'It was here, in the big world, that I would meet what I was waiting for.' Other literary allusions and references echo the earlier novels on this theme, as when Gabriel half-quotes Kepler's ideal, 'I was after simplicity now, the pure uncluttered thing.' Although Gabriel's relation to the astronomers is signalled by lines such as these, neither his character nor the narrative which expresses the development of that character is as convincing as the earlier versions of this ambitious fictional adventure.

The most effective and most original element of this part of the novel comes from Banville's precise poetic evocation of a disembodied malevolence which, like Felix, pursues and haunts Gabriel:

> The feeling was so strong I began to think I was being followed, as if really some flickering presence had materialized behind me. I would stop in the street and turn quickly, and at once everything would assume a studied air of innocence, the shopfronts and facades of houses looking suspiciously flat and insubstantial, like a hastily erected stage-set. (186)

Gabriel's imagination, released from fact and abstraction, now animates everything he sees. This paranoid sensitivity to the malevolent personality of the city is the price of that release, as if the spirit, if not the person, of Felix was alive in the very brickwork of the seemingly inert city. Personal tragedy and pain revolutionise the familiar world, making it at once exquisitely precious and remote. *Mefisto* is a radical example of Banville's way of mythologising the ordinary through a perception heightened by suffering.

Swan's narrative concludes by recalling a pattern of failure and tragedy which leaves him alone with a haunted memory and a book to write. Kosok's computer-scheme is abandoned, Adele dies from an overdose and Felix plans to move on from the debris he helped create. The macabre events in the city seem like a sadistic replay of Swan's earlier days at Ashburn. Writing about his suffering is not so much a consolation as an exorcism. Like Godkin, he is a refugee trying to recreate a life without meaning or compensation, and in a form doomed to misunderstanding. His fiction is just that, an imposition of fancy upon experience, inadequate but irresistible:

> Have I tied up all the ends? Even an invented world has its rules, tedious, absurd perhaps, but not to be gainsaid. (234)

Despite the grim pessimism of Gabriel's 'black book', a hesitant pledge is made in its final lines which recalls the novel's opening. He says that 'In future, I will leave things, I will try to leave things, to chance.' Like *Birchwood*, *Mefisto* is a back-to-front account: its cryptic opening is a conclusion waiting to be demonstrated. The enclosed circular pattern of the memoir has a symmetry inspired by terrified doubt or, to put it in his own terms, by a conviction that the seeming pattern of order is, on closer inspection, a conspiracy of chance and calamity. The meaning of Swan's story is foreshadowed by the phenomenon of twins which, like his subsequent experience of the world, is a mysterious complicity of design and accident.

Mefisto, as I have indicated, is a difficult and not wholly satisfying conclusion to Banville's own design. Much of this problem lies with the character of Gabriel Swan. His precocious talent for mathematical speculation gives him an initial token association with the classic astronomers. But once the novel becomes a kind of intellectual horror story, this gift never develops, as it did in the previous fictions, into a consuming passion. Given the form of *Mefisto*, such latent genius has no place in which to develop. The encounters with Kasperl and Kosok show a fascinated child-observer, but one who never actually works at his obsession. The painstaking drama of the astronomers' work never finds a corresponding force in *Mefisto*, whose 'scientific' theme is asserted but never fully realised.[7]

It might be argued, however, that Banville tried to write a very different kind of novel from one we expect in such a plan, while retaining some of its themes. This is true, as *Mefisto* has more in common with the self-conscious conventions of *Nightspawn* than with any other work by Banville, especially in its gallery of human oddities, its reckless episodic plot, and a heavy, sometimes intrusive, framework of literary allusion. Both novels suffer from carefully planned obscurity. *Mefisto* has some great moments, and Banville's descriptive style is as poetically precise and daring as ever, but overall the novel does not successfully blend the design of *Nightspawn*, the narrative form of *Birchwood*, and the purpose of the tetralogy. It is, in some ways, too clever, perhaps a fictional victim of that complication which sometimes prevents Banville's characters themselves from expressing 'the pure, uncluttered thing'.

8

The Book of Evidence

> But now crime has degraded me beneath the meanest animal. No guilt, no mischief, no malignity, no misery, can be found comparable to mine. When I run over the frightful catalogue of my sins, I cannot believe that I am the same creature whose thoughts were once filled with sublime and transcendent visions of the beauty and the majesty of goodness. But it is even so; the fallen angel becomes a malignant devil.
>
> Mary Shelley, *Frankenstein*

WITH *The Book of Evidence*, Banville produced a 'supreme fiction' which attracted greater critical interest and respect than any of his previous novels.[1] Nearly a decade beforehand, he had spoken of his readers as 'that small band': now his reputation was internationalised. His patient, attentive and imaginative craft had finally produced an extraordinary novel which harmonised his favourite fictions into a classic form of modern tragedy.

Like Dostoyevsky's *Crime and Punishment*, or Camus's *The Outsider*, Banville's novel explores an evil personality and the personality of Evil. Each of these novels is based on the casual and brutal murder of an innocent: unlike these other versions of the irrational, however, *The Book of Evidence* openly attributes the horrific deed to failure of the imagination. Freddie Montgomery, the confessional narrator who offers a subjective version of the case against him, may be seen as a subtle and complex personification of the figure who haunted, but never appeared in, *Long Lankin*. Freddie's passionate script, written to illustrate, not explain, is also similar to that by Gabriel Godkin in *Birchwood*, a memoir to banish ghosts and console him in his refuge. Above all, his disillusionment with scientific knowledge and his belated wonder at the beauty and mystery of the innocent phenomenal world, draws on the thematic strength of the astronomical tetralogy. This is a fiction about fiction; it is also one about its own fictional lineage. Yet this self-conscious allusiveness does not explain the novel's most distinctive and original embellishment — painting as a metaphor for nature's speechless and deceptive familiarity. Banville's contemplative fiction has finally discovered what it always knew — that the immediate, sensuous and commonplace world, seen through an estranged imagination, is the greatest mystery of all.

Such a revelation requires Freddie Montgomery's exclusion from the ordinary world. His narrative takes the form of a prison-memoir written to account for his identity and crime, a tale to be later placed alongside what he calls the 'official fictions'. Throughout the novel, Banville tries to give the illusion of spontaneous composition to his narrator's fictional script, with Freddie ever-sensitive to the misinterpretation of his story by judge, jury and 'amateur psychologists'. He repeatedly expresses weariness with his invention, even disgust, but is determined to see what his past might offer. The nostalgic structure of his evidence involves much more than simple motivation or culpability: now imprisoned like some 'exotic animal', he offers an imaginative autobiography of a man who foolishly believed in freedom.

The style of his story intensifies the artificial character of the imagined past, as if he can now see that he had always been an unwitting actor in a version of his life scripted by someone else. His recollections begin with a holiday which he and his wife, Daphne, spent on a Mediterranean island, enjoying a way of life which 'encouraged' illusions. In a witty amusing scenario full of cinematic stereotypes, Freddie recalls his casual and fatal involvement with the drug underworld. Blackmailed by a local baron, he returns home to find the money owed to the syndicate. A dream-like voyage takes him back to Ireland, where he immediately sets off to his ancestral home, the Big House estate at Coolgrange, a family-ruin inhabited by his distracted mother. In a series of drunken, operatic confrontations, he discovers that she cannot help him financially, having sold all the valuable paintings that formerly graced the walls of the house. Rejected by his mother and haunted by the memory of his perversely eccentric father, he feels that his dilemma resembles that 'same old squabble: money and betrayal'. But he quickly finds out that the paintings have passed through the hands of a wealthy neighbouring family, the Behrens, and he makes a frantic visit to retrieve his fancied inheritance. While wandering around the house, he is fascinated by one particular painting, an anonymous, mid-seventeenth-century Dutch work, entitled 'Portrait of a Woman with Gloves'.[2] He returns the next day and, in the act of stealing the painting, is interrupted by a young maid, Josie Bell, whom he abducts. Soon after, he beats the young woman to death with a hammer. The painting is abandoned and he goes to Dublin, where he renews an acquaintance with Charlie French, an old family friend, who offers him shelter without any questions. Freddie's last few days of refuge are spent in reckless and tormented self-indulgence, until the police arrive and arrest him. Only when he is finally manacled, does he feel free of the burdensome mask he has worn for so long.

This is the plot of Freddie's story, summarised with a continuity that does not yet take into account the many imaginative digressions and interruptions which weave themselves across such a frenzied sequence, and which give the narrative its yearning quality. Easily and willingly captivated by the images and faces conjured up by his inquisitive memory, he builds up a series of 'sub-texts', which seem to signify more than the facts of the plot. For example, we learn that he was once a lecturer in science at an American university, determined to 'be one of those great, cold technicians, the secret masters of the world'. In California he had met two women from Ireland, Daphne and Anna, had married the former, later realising he was secretly in love with the latter. (A similar regretful 'troilism' is seen also in

The Newton Letter.) The next time he meets Anna is when he comes looking for the paintings. By a studied coincidence, she is a neighbour, daughter of the Behrens family. There is a strong sense that the lady in the portrait awakens his memory of Anna, and hence attracts his hypnotised attention.

These stories within the main narrative seem to provide Freddie with the real evidence for his guilt. Memory suddenly perceives patterns, coincidences and designs which he was blind to at the time, but which now reveal a sinister, predetermined order to his fateful existence. The logic of these subconscious designs, now laid bare, confirms his feeling that the murder was premeditated but not intentional.

A fiction about the criminal mind is also one about the system of order being challenged. 'Law and order' in this novel may be seen as an earthly, and political, version of the scientific system of absolutes by which the human, everyday order is interpreted. Banville's aesthetic always interrogates these abstract codes of belief through the counter-evidence of a poetic sensibility. It may be shocking, therefore, but hardly surprising, that Freddie Montgomery finally claims that 'failure of imagination is my real crime, the one that made the others possible'.

In a fiction dominated by images of art, Freddie's guilt is rendered aesthetic, a more profoundly human charge than the legal one he has always accepted. The law's understanding of motive never comes near the final imaginative understanding of his own animalism. The legal system and process of inquisition are a great source of entertainment to Freddie, because they will only state the obvious, and do so in a language that could never describe the ghastly irrational personality of most human behaviour. The law's version of innocence and guilt produces only a snickering parody from Freddie:

> I realised that I had done the things I did because I could do no other. Please, do not imagine, my lord, I hasten to

say it, do not imagine that you detect here the insinuation of an apologia, or even of a defence. I wish to claim full responsibility for my actions—after all, they are the only things I can call my own—and I declare in advance that I shall accept without demur the verdict of the court. I am merely asking, with all respect, whether it is feasible to hold on to the principle of moral culpability once the notion of free will has been abandoned. It is, I grant you, a tricky one, the sort of thing we love to discuss in here of an evening, over our cocoa and our fags, when time hangs heavy. (16)

This is precisely the kind of philosophical conundrum that Nietzsche, in examining the innocent element in supposedly evil actions, held up to bourgeois morality.[3] Rationalism, it is argued, wrongly assumes a free subject behind violent acts of this kind. Reduced to his 'natural' state, Freddie now scrutinises the language of 'evil', and finds that it never quite matches his understanding. It usually implies a freedom that never existed: or it judges, without imagination, a hopelessly inadequate version of events. The morality of the law is as mystifying as its language. Like Camus's Meursault, Freddie never expresses regret or sorrow, and is thus confirmed as an inhuman monster: both characters also look forward to the spectacle of public retribution. But Freddie realises that his crime is greater than anyone imagines, and he refuses to act out emotions expected or required by the court, precisely because such a display may only encourage clemency. No system is necessary to prove what he already knows:

> The deed was done, and would not be cancelled by cries of anguish and repentance. Done, yes, finished, as nothing ever before in my life had been finished and done—and yet there would be no end to it, I saw that straight away. I was, I told myself, responsible, with all the weight that word implied. In killing Josie Bell I had

destroyed a part of the world. Those hammer-blows had shattered a complex of memories and sensations and possibilities—a life, in short—which was irreplaceable, but which, somehow, must be replaced. (151-2)

He declares that his own 'symbolic death' at the hands of the law may be necessary, even desirable, but Josie Bell must be 'brought back to life' in his own mind. His careless murder can be atoned for only by facing what was previously unimaginable.

Freddie's crime is explained, not excused, by an inherited schizophrenia which determined actions he had mistaken for choices. He was always a marionette, never a free man. Prison, in this sense, is a homecoming. Through his narrator's experience, Banville tries to dramatise an existential sense of the theatricality of rational behaviour, a life spent denying the reality of chance and the power of the demonic self. To avoid substituting the abstractions of psychology for those of philosophy, Banville creates a pattern of biographical detail which 'explains' Freddie's confusion in terms of familiar, often farcical, fictions. Stereotypes and clichés are indispensable to this kind of absurdism. Outrageous and exotic names are a favoured contrivance in suggesting the unreal, staged quality of Freddie's new world, such as the lavish Gaelic of his barrister, Maolseachlin Mac Giolla Gunna, or the allegorical nastiness of his interrogators, Kickham and Barker. Nothing seems funnier, or more touching, than the seriousness with which the law takes Freddie. Its comic pretensions never fail to tickle him.

Equally playful, but more profound, is the fatal imprint of genetic inheritance, a recurrent motif in Banville. Family, parents and childhood suddenly seem crucial. Son of a father who prided himself on being a 'Castle Catholic' (who insisted on the colonial name 'Kingstown' instead of the nationalist 'Dun Laoghaire'), and a mother descended from 'King Billy's henchmen', even his immediate family seems like a violation or betrayal of nature and convention. Looking back on his solitary childhood, he now sees the tragic dualism of his personality: outside, the cultured intelligent son of the Big House, but inside, a violent sadistic brute trying to be free, a monster he names 'Bunter'. On the day of the crime, he recalls, 'Bunter was restive, aching to get out.' In a sense only appreciated by Freddie, the wrong self has been arrested. After the murder, the triumph of evil is recalled by Freddie with grim, fascinated acceptance:

> Now I had struck a blow for the inner man, that guffawing, fat foulmouth who had been telling me all along I was living a lie. And he had burst out at last, it was he, the ogre, who was pounding along in this lemon-coloured light, with blood on his pelt, and me slung helpless over his back. Everything was gone, the past, Coolgrange, Daphne, all my previous life, gone, abandoned, drained of its essence, its significance. To do the worst thing, the very worst thing, that's the way to be free. I would never again need to pretend to myself to be what I was not. (124–5)

Such sentiments are an affront to logic as well as to morality. Contrary to superstition, the 'inner man' turns out to be a devil, not an angel. But this is a subjective testimony based on emotion not reason, and Freddie's honesty limits itself to a personal sense of being at odds with the civilised world. His 'truth' is tentative, paradoxical and defiant. The only way he can overthrow or resist the pattern of his life and crime is through an imaginative effort. His only consolation is a belated acceptance of the significance of recollected images.

The implied solution to Freddie's crime lies in the relationship between two pictures — the Dutch portrait and a photo of Josie Bell. How are we to understand his obsessive attraction towards the painting? He was, so to speak, accidentally lured to the painting by the presence of Anna, his fantasy-woman. In prison, he recalls his first sighting of the portrait:

> You have seen the picture in the papers, you know what she looks like. A youngish woman in a black dress with a

broad white collar, standing with her hands folded in front of her, one gloved, the other hidden except for the fingers, which are flexed, ringless. She is wearing something on her head, a cap or clasp of some sort, which holds her hair drawn tightly back from her brow. Her prominent black eyes have a faintly oriental slant. The nose is large, the lips full. She is not beautiful. In her right hand she holds a folded fan, or it might be a book. She is standing in what I take to be the lighted doorway of a room. Part of a couch can be seen, or maybe a bed, with a brocade cover. The darkness behind her is dense and yet mysteriously weightless. Her gaze is calm, inexpectant, though there is a trace of challenge, of hostility, even, in the set of her mouth. She does not want to be here, and yet cannot be elsewhere. The gold brooch that secures the wings of her wide collar is expensive and ugly. All this you have seen, all this you know. Yet I put it to you, gentle connoisseurs of the jury, that even knowing all this you still know nothing, next to nothing. You do not know the fortitude and pathos of her presence. You have not come upon her suddenly in a golden room on a summer eve, as I have. You have not held her in your arms, you have not seen her asprawl in a ditch. You have not—ah no!—you have not killed for her. (78–9)

The woman in the painting recalls Anna and foreshadows Josie Bell. His last image of Anna, when leaving America, was of her standing by a window, framed by the light. (Fifteen years later, she now appears, 'like one of Klimt's gem-encrusted lovers'.) Sneaking the portrait out of her house, he is interrupted by the maid 'standing in the open french window'. While in hiding, he sees a photo of Josie Bell in the newspaper 'gazing out solemn-eyed from a blurred background ... she was wearing a long ugly dress with an elaborate collar, and was clutching something, flowers, perhaps, in her hands'. The accidental encounters with Anna and Josie are 'framed' in the anonymous work of art, in a way that Freddie appreciates but does not comprehend. The real artist behind the portrait might be said to be Freddie himself who, looking at a reproduction of the picture (a gift from Anna) in his prison-cell, creates an elaborate and detailed fantasy about the possible background to the portrait. He imagines an old Dutch merchant commissioning a portrait of his only daughter, who reluctantly agrees to sit for a picture which the father hopes will immortalise his beloved child. In this fantasy, Freddie is fascinated by the sensuous texture of the artist's chaotic and foul-smelling studio, and with the young woman's nervous and sceptical presence. When the painting is completed, the woman is enthralled—'She had expected it would be like looking in a mirror, but this is someone she does not recognise, and yet knows.' Numbed with happiness, she 'steps out into a commonplace world'. That world, unfortunately, is the one that Josie Bell inhabits.

Freddie is willing and able to summon up the world behind the work of art, an image of distant repose, but he cannot see Josie Bell's 'commonplace world'. The background to the photo is 'blurred', whereas the setting of the portrait is described with much more confidence and with a certain voyeuristic relish. Freddie made up the story of the portrait's background because, in his own words, 'she was asking me to let her live'. If his crime is 'a failure of imagination', it is even more specifically traced to his blind contempt for the material world of class. A servant has been murdered by a master, albeit a displaced one. In a colonial context, it is also the murder of a 'native' by one of the Anglo-Irish.[4] Freddie recalls being led from the courthouse, and noticing the hostile crowd—'That was when I realised, for the first time, it was *one of theirs* I had killed.' Confessing his shame at having taken so long to beat her to death, he hears his barrister remark, 'Hardy people . . . they don't die easily.' Freddie's crime is part of a pattern of calculated cruelty in the novel, but his irrationality is mediated through the imagery of art in a way that suggests a disturbing link between culture and perception. He can see Anna Behrens in terms of the Dutch masters, or his mother as one of 'Lautrec's ruined doxies', but he cannot adequately picture Josie Bell's world. Only after the crime, and especially now when he no longer has to pretend, does he see the relation between perception and knowledge. The meaning of his evidence, he insists repeatedly, is to be sensed in its images. Fiction becomes his only hope.

As with so many of Banville's narrators, the shock to Freddie's imaginative system releases a previously unfelt sympathy for the imagery of innocence. Like the astronomers, he comes to feel an exquisite regret and wonder at having forgotten or ignored the obvious. He remembers wandering around Dublin after the murder, 'a quavering Dr Jekyll', as if he was seeing for the first time:

> I felt I had never until now looked at the ordinary world around me, the people, places, things. How innocent it all seemed, innocent, and doomed. How can I express the tangle of emotions that thrashed inside me as I prowled the city streets, letting my monstrous heart feed its fill on the sights and sounds of the commonplace? (172–3)

His crime against this innnocent world endears it to him, but also ensures his banishment from it. Every detail of the world's texture suddenly seems precious and tragic when viewed for the first and last time. Like Gabriel Swan, Freddie is an emblem of deformed and, therefore, 'true' humanity. This is why he pursues the freaks of Dublin's nightlife, the 'maimed and the mad', who now seem to him the very epitome of his own sad race. In scenes which recall the final episodes of *Mefisto*, Freddie discovers a community of tormented souls like himself, and can only feel pity and amazement at their survival.

The greatest artistic challenge that faces Banville is to persuade us that Freddie is, somehow, innocent. Such a stylistic sleight of hand is achieved through this myth of a nature damaged at birth, after which only glimpses of harmony are possible. Freddie is a poetic animal, not a fallen angel. Prison is the obvious, even traditional, metaphor for such an intelligent beast who realises that sanity requires an unbearable degree of mimicry. Once housed in jail, the artifice can be dispensed with and his true nature released. As he slyly remarks, 'To place all faith in the mask, that seems to me now the true stamp of refined humanity.' Prison reduces existence to a simpler, more meaningful equation of good and evil, guilt and innocence, and provides Freddie with a perfect vantage point from which he can see the world in its authentic innocence. It also liberates the lyricist in him. The cell window provides him with a barred frame through which he watches, and is watched by, the ordinary world of sky and tree. This miniaturist perspective on the world is all he needs; his imagination will do the rest.

Reality, whether that of the prison or the outside world, always comes as a surprise to Freddie. His fanciful notions of what to expect usually prove embarrassing or ludicrous. Yet it is often these very delusions, once confessed, which bring him a revitalised and self-critical understanding. The story's sense of the absurd comes from his ability to watch himself and others behave like poor actors, all the time thinking they are free and purposeful. This is the art and humour of existential bathos. Now free to watch himself, he recalls his surprise on first entering prison: his 'hopelessly romantic' expectations of jail led him to picture himself as 'Jean-Jacques the cultured killer', but the reality has an unforeseen elusiveness and originality which subvert the imaginative script. Forever looking for the wrong kind of melodrama in the wrong place, he soon sees that 'in here is like out there, only more so'. Without theatrical roles, the world would come to a silent standstill. Most of the players in his story can be memorised only in terms of an exotic farce which cannot distinguish between the natural and the contrived. Playing comic roles seriously is the greatest source of derisive humour for Freddie. His pursuit and arrest now seem worthy of a Hollywood thriller, with the police smashing their way into the house, only to find the psychopath having supper. The many lurid versions of his appearance offered by eye-witnesses now seem to him 'like a chorus of brigands in an Italian opera'. Freddie's satirical imagination is now one of his favourite pastimes.

Not everything is reduced to farce by this imagination. There are moments in his evidence when Freddie glimpses images of rare silent beauty which overwhelm him, as if this fallen, demented world still preserves traces of perfection, like fossils of lost harmony. Normally his imagination leaves him floundering, only confirmed in his sense of the unbridgeable discrepancy between hope and reality. Yet, occasionally, as if some authentic script had been prepared for him without his knowing, he is the enraptured witness to the poetry of experience. Usually this revelation occurs in the least poetic of circumstances, as if beauty is the gift of genuine surprise. This mystical, idealistic strain is present in nearly all of Banville's fiction, and is protected from an easy assertive romanticism by a sense of the pain and absurdity necessary to experience it. Freddie's imagistic memory is particularly attracted to those interludes of calm which seem to symbolise some divine artistry in the natural world:

> I had expected to arrive in rain, and at Holyhead, indeed, a fine, warm drizzle was falling, but when we got out on the channel the sun broke through again. It was evening. The sea was calm, an oiled, taut meniscus, mauve-tinted and curiously high and curved. From the forward lounge where I sat the prow seemed to rise and rise, as if the whole ship were straining to take to the air. The sky before us was a smear of crimson on the palest of pale blue and silvery green. I held my face up to the calm sea-light, entranced, expectant, grinning like a loon. I confess I was not entirely sober, I had already broken into my allowance of duty-free booze, and the skin at my temples and around my eyes was tightening alarmingly.

> It was not just the drink, though, that was making me happy, but the tenderness of things, the simple goodness of the world. This sunset, for instance, how lavishly it was laid on, the clouds, the light on the sea, that heartbreaking, blue-green distance, laid on, all of it, as if to console some lost, suffering wayfarer. (26)

It is that sense of nature being 'laid on' which captures Freddie's animistic imagination, as if an invisible landscape artist had arranged the scene especially for him. The world becomes an aesthetic and fictional production, all the more beautiful for being carefully rehearsed. What gives moments like this their distinctive poignancy is the inclusion of sad, human detail, some contrasting image of earthly insignificance. It is as if a utopian simplicity of design has suddenly been noticed, a world which retains its purity and form, and which silently observes the lunatic antics of the fallen world. These intimations of beauty are always prompted by the commonplace, but especially by silence. Very little is ever spoken in Banville's fiction. When people speak they usually spoil the silence, or ruin an expectation. One evening in Charlie French's house, while his nervous host is doing the washing-up with a cigarette dangling from his lip, Freddie watches him and notices the pale indigo sky through the kitchen window—'I thought I had never seen anything so lovely in my life.' Even though everything quickly resorts to its farcical nature, such compositional moments give his story its poetic life.

Through the motif of painting, Banville has discovered a series of metaphors that are perfectly in harmony with his poetic fiction. Intelligent but anti-intellectual, scholarly but sceptical, such fiction always returns to the sensuous image for expressive meaning. The silent image bypasses language to appeal directly to the heart and the subconscious mind. As with masks, Freddie comes to trust only externals, since, he concludes, 'that's where there is depth'. Viewed this way, appearances are everything. As Freddie's pictorial imagination understands it, images can retain an honesty which words will only confuse. Of course, the most teasing paradox about all this is that Banville's language, so metaphoric and precise, should have the stylistic confidence to convey a story which denies the adequacy of language. Freddie himself finally expresses this ironic achievement:

> I had Daphne bring me big thick books on Dutch painting, not only the history but the techniques, the secrets of the masters. I studied accounts of the methods of grinding colours, of the trade in oils and dyes, of the flax industry in Flanders. I read the lives of the painters and their patrons. I became a minor expert on the Dutch republic in the seventeenth century. But in the end it was no good: all this learning, this information, merely built up and petrified, like coral encrusting a sunken wreck. (214)

Even failure and ignorance, as captured in that final inspired analogy, have precious aesthetic value when acknowledged by the liberated imagination.

Like Newton, but this time through a very different set of metaphors, Freddie sees systematised knowledge as an illusory distraction from an earthly order which was watching him all the time, waiting to be noticed. Other echoes of the astronomers' experience are woven into this new design, most significantly the ideas of perception and perspective. Freddie, like his fictional relations in the tetralogy, finds a new way of looking at the familiar world, a place whose beauty is evident only to those who accept their own insignificance. In the old order of things, man placed himself at the centre of the universe, master of all he surveyed. Now, that order is reversed, and the universe includes man in its silent, pitiful gaze. The astronomer in Freddie offers a metaphysical conceit to describe this tragic confusion:

> I have never really got used to being on this earth. Sometimes I think our presence here is due to a cosmic blunder, that we were meant for another planet

altogether, with other arrangements, and other laws, and other, grimmer skies. I try to imagine it, our true place, off on the far side of the galaxy, whirling and whirling. And the ones who were meant for here, are they out there, baffled and homesick, like us? No, they would have become extinct long ago. How could they survive, these gentle earthlings, in a world that was made to contain *us*? (26–7)

An ingenious parable of perception, *The Book of Evidence* completes Banville's vision of a de-centred universe in which man protects and consoles himself through his fabulous imagination.

9
Conclusion

In those stern taut stories that comprise *Long Lankin*, Banville seized upon the 'displaced persons set' as a medium through which he could express a social sense of existential *Angst*. The motif of the outsider has retained its importance throughout the subsequent fiction, but has been invested with a mythological dimension which transforms individual alienation into an imaginative drama of evil and redemption. The literary and astronomical designs within the novels give them a classical perspective on man's place in nature. Banville's fiction has developed its own poetic myth of displacement, whereby the earth feels like the wrong home for its inhabitants, who forever look to an imaginative heaven for their lost security. Kepler thinks of those 'sad stunted creatures' on the moon, wayward earthlings, stranded in space and time, just as Freddie Montgomery feels that a terrible 'cosmic blunder' has condemned humanity to everlasting exile. Such a perspective has a shocking effect on Banville's narrators, who see greater intensity of life in the phenomenal world than in themselves. The 'inanimate' world always overwhelms them with its human properties, as if mocking the lifeless antics of the inhabitants. Banville's fiction has a creative obsession with this alarmed sense of duality, a tension between opposites which stare each other into acceptance and recognition. Like the Manichaean heresy, Banville's world is one dominated by a perverse God who enjoys tormenting his subjects: but it is also a world which retains signs of another compassionate and magical divinity. Faced with such an elemental drama of faith and despair, of knowledge and ignorance, Banville's narrators, once their fictional burdens are complete, discover that a wordless silence is the most eloquent version of their lost potential.

Those narrators, always men, talk and write too much, to the point where they must begin again to watch and listen. Women, who play such a silent role in the novels, embody a myth of intuitive wisdom and grace always lamented by those 'high cold heroes', those 'great cold technicians' of the ambitious mind. This most fundamental opposition suggests that the tragedy of this fiction is as much one of the masculine personality as of the intellect.

Notes

Introduction (1–12)
1. See, my article, 'An Exalted Naming: The Poetical Fictions of John Banville', *The Canadian Journal of Irish Studies*, July 1988, vol xiv, no i, 17–27.
2. *The Theory of the Novel*, translated by Anna Bostock, Merlin Press, London, 1971, 88.
3. *The Novelist at the Crossroads*, Routledge & Kegan Paul, London, 1971, 33. A lucid and lively account of trends in modern fiction, especially those in England and America.
4. *Possibilities*, Oxford University Press, London, 1973, 24. See especially, part one, 'The Open Form: The Novel and Reality', 3–30.
5. *The Modes of Modern Writing*, Edward Arnold, London, 1977, 240. On the question of language, Lodge argues that modernist fiction tends towards the poetic, especially the metaphoric. Much of this analysis is based on Jakobson's theories of modern stylistics, for which see, 74–81.
6. 'Q & A with John Banville', by Rüdiger Imhof, *Irish Literary Supplement*, spring 1987, 13.
7. See, my article, 'Stereotypical Images of Ireland in John Banville's Fiction', *Éire–Ireland*, xxiii, 3, fall 1988, 94–102.
8. See, Banville's comments on the use of this genre in *Birchwood*, *Irish University Review*, John Banville Special Issue, spring 1981, 11.
9. 'Out of Chaos Comes Order', an interview by Ciaran Carty, *The Sunday Tribune*, 14 September 1986.
10. *Irish University Review*, 14.
11. See 'Novelists on the Novel', *The Crane Bag*, MP Hederman and R Kearney eds, Blackwater Press, Dublin, 1982, 408f, in which Banville and Francis Stuart are interviewed by Ronan Sheehan on the question of tradition and its significance for the Irish writer.
12. *Transitions*, Wolfhound Press, Dublin, 1987, 98–100.
13. 'Kenner's Joyce', review-article, *The Irish Times*, 17 June 1989.
14. In a tribute to Beckett, who had died in Paris only days

beforehand, see, *The Irish Times*, 23 December 1989, 19. For a longer version of this piece, see, 'Waiting for the last Word', *The Observer*, 31 December 1989, 36.
15. *Irish University Review*, 17.
16. 'Wexford', *32 Counties—Photographs of Ireland*, Donovan Wylie, Martin Secker & Warburg, London, 1989, 200.
17. In language very similar to that used by Banville, the critic Declan Kiberd has argued that Ireland is a 'necessary fiction' for many Irish writers, precisely because any satisfying idea of 'the true republic' in which the idea of the nation would be embodied in the state, has yet to be fulfilled. See, his chapter, 'Irish Literature and Irish History', *The Oxford Illustrated History of Ireland*, RF Foster ed, Oxford University Press, 1989, 275–337, especially 334–7.
18. 'A novel seems to be as if you had sat down and taken three or four years to explain a dream to someone in such a way that they could experience the weight or power of the dream that you did.' *The Sunday Tribune*. See also, 'Stepping into the limelight— and the chaos', *The Irish Times*, 21 October 1989, an interview with Fintan O'Toole, written just before the Booker Prize and the GPA award. Here, Banville says, 'I've always likened writing a novel to having a powerful dream that you know is going to haunt you for days.' He adds, 'Maybe that's why I've never been particularly well understood in England: they assume I'm trying to write a traditional English novel and failing, whereas I'm not trying to write that at all. Now, maybe they're right, maybe the novel shouldn't be turned into something that could have the same density and concentration that poetry strives for. But I'm not interested in writing anything else.'
19. For example, in reviewing Paul Auster's *The New York Trilogy*, Banville finds its multiple allusiveness 'clever, and interesting, in a dry sort of way; it is also, however, one of the faults of the trilogy. A text as relentlessly referential as this can have no true, proper, *organic* life of its own.' *The Irish Times*, 24 January 1988.
20. *The Aesthetic Dimension*, Macmillan Press, London, 1979, 68.

Long Lankin (13–20)
1. For the complete text see, *The Penguin Book of English Folk Songs*, RV Williams, AL Lloyd eds, Penguin, London, 1976, 60–61.
2. 'An Interview with John Banville', Rüdiger Imhof, *Irish University Review*, 9.
3. A point made by Rüdiger Imhof in 'Banville's Supreme Fiction',

Irish University Review, 55. But the stories are not, as Imhof argues, arranged along the same categories as Joyce's *Dubliners*.
4. *Long Lankin*, Martin Secker & Warburg, London, 1970, 99. All references are to this edition.
5. 'An Interview with John Banville', 8.
6. *Long Lankin*, Gallery Press, Dublin, 1984.
7. Lucretius, Roman poet and philosopher, wrote his lengthy poem in praise of Epicurus, arguing that the pleasures offered to the senses by the natural world were the only proper aim of human existence. The first of many classical allusions in Banville's fiction.
8. 'Stepping into the limelight—and the chaos'.

Nightspawn (21–29)
1. Michael Denning, *Cover Stories*, Routledge & Kegan Paul, London, 1987, 2.
2. *Nightspawn*, Martin Secker & Warburg, London, 1971, 7. All references are to this edition.
3. The passage recalls the opening lines of *Notes from Underground*, and alludes to Keats's verse-tragedy, *Isabella, or The Pot of Basil*, a version of the story from Boccaccio.
4. 'An Interview with John Banville', *Irish University Review*, 5.
5. '"Be Assured I Am Inventing": The Fiction of John Banville', *The Irish Novel in our Time*, P Rafroidi and M Harmon eds, Lille, 1975, 334. One of the earliest and still one of the best articles on Banville.
6. 'An Interview with John Banville', 6.
7. ibid, 6–7.
8. In the Greek myth, out of the blood of the slain youth grew a beautiful flower, hence the name, and its association here with 'Flora'.

Birchwood (30–45)
1. 'An Interview with John Banville', 11.
2. See, Rüdiger Imhof's *John Banville: A Critical Introduction*, Wolfhound, Dublin, 1989, 53–73, for detailed discussion of genres. Imhof emphasises the formal intricacy of the novel, its 'wheels-within-wheels' design.
3. *Birchwood*, first published by Martin Secker & Warburg, London,

1973. Here from Granada edition, London, 1984, 12. All references are to this edition.
4. For background to myth, see, AJ Spencer, *Death in Ancient Egypt*, Penguin, London, 1982, 142–51.
5. An 'outlandish alias' because it is, not surprisingly, an anagram for 'John Banville'.
6. 'Aire and Angels', from which the following lines suggest something of the exalted quality which Banville tries to create in this section:

> Then as an Angell, face and wings
> Of aire, not pure as it, yet pure doth weare,
> So thy love may be my loves spheare;
> Just such disparitie
> As is twixt Aire and Angells puritie,
> 'Twixt womens love, and mens will ever be.

See, *John Donne—Selected Poems*, John Hayward ed, Penguin, London, 1977, 36. Note also Donne's use of astronomical metaphor to suggest the mysteries of love: in its inventiveness and daring, Banville's use of imagery is often 'metaphysical'.
7. Nabokov's *Ada* seems like a strong presence in *Birchwood*. Subtitled, 'A Family Chronicle', its central characters are also twins. Nabokov's equally self-conscious narrator is fascinated, like Gabriel, by the fictions of time, saying 'I am also aware that Time is a fluid medium for the culture of metaphors'.
8. David Lodge finds that sexual ambiguity is a favourite and recurrent motif in much of this kind of writing: 'One of the most emotively powerful emblems of contradiction, one that affronts the most fundamental binary system of all, is the hermaphrodite; and it is not surprising that the characters of post-modernist fiction are often sexually ambivalent.' See, his *Modes of Modern Writing*, 229. His examples include Gore Vidal's *Myra Breckinridge* and John Barth's *Giles Goat-boy*.
9. 'Looking for Pure Visions', *Graph*, first issue, Dublin, October 1986, 14–15.
10. '"Be Assured I Am Inventing": The Fiction of John Banville', 333.
11. See, Richard Kearney, *Transitions*, Wolfhound, Dublin 1988, 91–3, on the epistemological questions raised by these two 'philosophers of modern European doubt', as he calls them. The line from Wittgenstein is taken from the *Tractatus Logico-Philosophicus*, 5.6.
12. 'An Interview with John Banville', 11.

Doctor Copernicus (46–67)
1. Arthur Koestler, *The Sleepwalkers*, Hutchinson, London, 1979; Thomas Kuhn, *The Copernican Revolution*, Harvard University Press, Cambridge, Mass, 1976. While both books deal with astronomical theory, Koestler is more concerned with the individual personality and its creative dimension.
2. ibid, 124.   3. ibid. 191–5.   4. ibid. 135.
5. For Koestler, this fear seems as much a question of personality as conviction. See, 153–65.
6. ibid, 136.
7. Especially Goethe's *Faust*, in its dramatisation of ambition and corruption through Faust and Mephistopheles, a relationship echoed in that between Copernicus and his brother, Andreas. But Thomas Mann's version of the myth, *Doktor Faustus*, seems to me just as important, a novel which provides many references and allusions in Banville's tetralogy, and whose protagonist, the musician, Adrian, in his obsession with the symbolic language of musical harmonies, offers an interesting comparison with Banville's astronomer. On the question of Goethe, see, Imhof's article, 'German Influences on John Banville and Aidan Higgins', *Literary Interrelations—Ireland, England and the World*, Wolfgang Zach and Heinz Kosok eds, Gunter Narr Verlag, Tübingen, 1987, vol 2, 335–47, in which he concentrates on Goethe's influence on *The Newton Letter*. He does not, surprisingly, deal with Thomas Mann. Banville himself, however, has spoken of Mann's novel as 'a presence behind all four books in the series'. See, 'Q & A with John Banville', 13.
8. *Doctor Copernicus*, first published by Martin Secker & Warburg, London, 1976, 13. The text used here is that by Granada, London, 1980. All references are to this edition.
9. On the orthodoxy of such fictions, see, P Machamer, 'Fictionalism and Realism in 16th Century Astronomy', *The Copernican Achievement*, R Westman ed, Univ of California Press, London, 1975, 346–53.
10. For Imhof's views on the centrality of language to this novel, see, his *John Banville—A Critical Introduction*, 74–9.
11. ibid, 132. The image of Andreas as a 'leper' accords well with Banville's motif of the outsider in *Long Lankin*.
12. cf. Thomas Mann's Adrian, whose Latin phrase, 'Noli me tangere' (Do not touch me), epitomises his aloofness.
13. That suffering, especially sickness, deepens the character, is

central to Nietzsche's thought. See, *Thus Spoke Zarathustra*, Penguin, London, 1961, introduction by RJ Hollingdale, 18.
14. For the story of Rheticus's: historical role, see, Koestler, 153–90.
15. For details of this important transfer of control, and the question of Copernicus's possible connivance in the affair, see, Koestler, 166f, and Kuhn, 187f.
16. Koestler, 167.
17. See, Kuhn, 196f, for background to these political and religious issues and how they shaped the public reception of the heliocentric theory.
18. *Keats: Poetical Works*, HW Garrod ed, Oxford, 1970, 210.
19. Mann's novel also begins and concludes with the childhood image of the linden tree.
20. *Wallace Stevens: Selected Poems*, Faber, London, 1980, 99. Banville's novel is rich in allusion to and quotation from this poem.

Kepler (68–87)
1. For an account of Kepler's scientific discoveries, see, Thomas Kuhn's *The Copernican Revolution*, 209–19. An important imaginative, as well as technical, source is, once again, Koestler's *The Sleepwalkers*.
2. For Imhof's detailed analysis of the novel's formal structures, see, his *John Banville—A Critical Introduction*, 131–8.
3. *Kepler*, first published in 1981 by Martin Secker & Warburg, London, 11. The text used here is by Granada, London, 1985. All references are to this edition.
4. Koestler contrasts Kepler, 'who came from a family of misfits', with Brahe, 'a grand seigneur from the Hamlet country', 283.
5. ibid, 266. He also characterises Kepler as a man who 'always remained a waif and a stray'.
6. When first published, Kepler added Rheticus's *Narratio Prima*, the summary of Copernicus's theory, as an appendix to the *Mysterium* in order to save readers from the unreadable. See, Koestler, 254.
7. For details of the original incident, and Kepler's comments, see, Koestler, 247f. Kepler remarked, 'I believe Divine Providence arranged matters in such a way that what I could not obtain with all my efforts was given to me through chance.'
8. See, Kuhn, 214–19. For Kepler, as Kuhn puts it, 'God's nature is mathematical.'
9. That imperative and suppliant voice is from Rilke's *Duino*

Elegies. The key passage, which also supplies the novel's epigraph, is one of Banville's most inspirational sources:
> Praise this world to the Angel, not the untellable: you can't impress him with the splendour you've felt; in the cosmos where he more feelingly feels you're only a novice. So show him some simple thing, refashioned by age after age, till it lives in our hands and eyes as a part of ourselves. Tell him things.

Duino Elegies, with English translation, introduction and commentary by JB Leishman and Stephen Spender, fourth edition, Chatto & Windus, London, 1981, 87.
10. From the 'Türmerlied' in Goethe's *Faust*:
> Ihr glücklichen Augen,
> Was je ihr gesehn,
> Es sei, wie es wolle,
> Es war doch so schön!

> Dear eyes, you so happy,
> Whatever you've seen,
> No matter its nature,
> So fair has it been!

For the fuller context, see, Goethe's *Faust*, translation and introduction by Philip Wayne, Penguin, London, 1971, 259–61.
11. ibid, 241.
12. In Mann's *Faustus*, Dürer is also Adrian's exemplary inspiration, especially the images of *Melancholia* and *Apocalypse*.
13. See, Koestler's commentary on this autobiographical fantasy, 415–19.

The Newton Letter (88–97)
1. *The Newton Letter*, first published in 1982, London, Martin Secker & Warburg. The edition used here is by Granada, 1984. All references are to this edition.
2. The full background to this incident can be read in RS Westfall's *Never at Rest: A Biography of Isaac Newton*, Cambridge, UP, Cambridge, 1980, 532–41.
3. For the complete text, see, *Selected Prose*, translated by M Hottinger and T and J Stern, with introduction by Hermann Broch, Routledge & Kegan Paul, London, 1952, 129–41, in which it appears as 'The Letter from Lord Chandos'.
4. *Graph*, 12–16. Imhof stresses the influence of Goethe's *Elective*

Affinities on the novella, especially in the choice of characters' names. See, his *Critical Introduction*, 145–7.
5. Just as the boy Gabriel, in *Birchwood*, faced with Justin and Juliette, those 'doubles in body and spirit', invents 'Justinette'.
6. Almost word for word from the original. See, *Selected Prose*, 140–41.
7. From the last line of 'The Ninth Elegy' in *Duino Elegies*, 89.
8. Based on an anecdotal remark made by Newton to a friend, shortly before his death. See, Westfall, 863.

Mefisto (98–108)
1. Banville has disclaimed any realistic intent in the early part of the tetralogy, saying that 'these astronomers were merely a means for me to speak of certain ideas, and to speak of them *in certain ways*. They also, of course, supplied readymade plots, which was handy.' 'Q & A with John Banville', 13.
2. See, Imhof's *Critical Introduction*, 153–70, for detailed comparisons between Goethe's *Faust* and *Mefisto*. This analysis was first published in his article, 'Swan's Way, or Goethe, Einstein, Banville—The Eternal Recurrence', *Études Irlandaises*, December 1987, no 12-2, 113–29.
3. Pressed on the correspondences between *Mefisto* and *Birchwood*, Banville says that this final novel of the series 'was returning to what one might call the realm of pure imagination out of which *Birchwood* was produced. No more history, no more facts!' 'Q & A with John Banville', 13.
4. In an interview on the eve of *Mefisto*'s publication, Banville mentioned this recurrent motif: 'There are things in fiction you do consciously and things you do because you couldn't help doing them. The notion of the lost self is something I can't help because I come back to it again and again.' 'Out of Chaos Comes Order', 18.
5. *Mefisto*, Martin Secker & Warburg, London, 1986, 8. All references are to this edition.
6. Interestingly, Keats's 'Lamia' is usually interpreted as a romantic attack upon the scientific and analytic mind.
7. Looking back on *Mefisto*, Banville himself expressed reservations about the form of the novel: 'A lot of things got into it that I didn't understand, but I let them stay. The book caused me terrible problems because I finished it with the technical problems unsolved. I didn't get the tone, but I was very proud of

having finished it in spite of not solving the problems.' 'Stepping into the limelight—and the chaos'.

The Book of Evidence (109–123)
1. *The Book of Evidence*, Martin Secker & Warburg, London, 1989. All references are to this edition. The French-language edition is *Le Livre Des Aveux*, translated by Michèle Albaret, Flammarion, Paris, 1990.
2. The names of Rembrandt, Frans Hals and Vermeer, according to Freddie, have been suggested as possible authors of the portrait. But he dismisses such speculative curiosity, saying that it is 'safer' to regard the work as 'anonymous'. There is no need to hunt down the painting or its author: I take the picture to be a fiction, but one closely inspired by artists like Vermeer, whose hypnotic portraits of women are worth consultation in this context. As a matter of small interest, other painters referred to in the novel include Van Gogh, Tintoretto, Fragonard and Lautrec. We might also note that the early seventeenth century, which saw a revolution in all kinds of perspective, is Kepler's age as well as that of the Dutch landscape and portrait artists. This is post-Reformation Europe, in which a new and necessary focus on the human landscape emerges.
3. In *Human, All Too Human* (1878), Nietschze writes: 'The evil acts at which we are now most indignant rest on the error that he who perpetrates them against us possesses free-will, that is to say, that he could have *chosen* not to cause us this harm. It is this belief in choice that engenders hatred, revengefulness, deceitfulness, complete degradation of the imagination, while we are far less censorious towards an animal because we regard it as unaccountable.' Here from *A Nietschze Reader*, selected, translated and introduced by RJ Hollingdale, Penguin, London, 1977, 76–7.
4. The 'accidental' killing in Camus' novel takes place in colonial Algiers. Meursault, Raskolnikov and Montgomery all murder someone below their own class: the civil servant kills an Arab, the student kills a pawnbroker, the scientist kills a servant.

Select Bibliography

Banville, John, 'A Talk', *Irish University Review*, John Banville Special Issue, vol 11, no 1, spring 1981, 13–17.
Carty, Ciaran, 'Out of Chaos Comes Order', *The Sunday Tribune*, 14 September 1986, 18.
Deane, Seamus, '"Be Assured I Am Inventing" — The Fiction of John Banville', *The Irish Novel in Our Time*, edited by P Rafroidi and M Harmon, Université de Lille, 1975, 329–38.
Donnelly, Brian, 'The Big House in the Recent Novel', *Studies*, 64, 1975, 133–42.
Imhof, Rüdiger, 'An Interview with John Banville', *Irish University Review*, 5–12.
Imhof, Rüdiger, 'John Banville's Supreme Fiction', *Irish University Review*, 52–86.
Imhof, Rüdiger, 'John Banville: A Checklist', *Irish University Review*, 87–95.
Imhof, Rüdiger, 'Swan's Way: or Goethe, Einstein, Banville — The Eternal Recurrence', *Études Irlandaises*, vol xii, no 2, 1987, 113–29.
Imhof, Rüdiger, 'German Influences on John Banville and Aidan Higgins', *Literary Interrelations: Ireland, England and the World*, edited by H Kosok and W Zach, vol 2, Tübingen, 1987, 335–48.
Imhof, Rüdiger, 'Q & A with John Banville', *Irish Literary Supplement*, spring, 1987, 13.
Imhof, Rüdiger, *John Banville: A Critical Introduction*, Wolfhound Press, Dublin, 1989.
Kearney, Richard, 'John Banville', *Transitions*, Wolfhound Press, Dublin, 1987, 91–100.
Kilroy, Thomas, 'Teller of Tales', *The Times Literary Supplement*, 17 March 1972, 301–2.
Lernout, Geert, 'Looking for Pure Visions', *Graph*, first issue, October 1986, 12–16.
McGonagle, Anthony, 'The Big House in John Banville's Fiction', unpublished MA thesis, University of Ulster, Jordanstown, 1989.

McMinn, Joseph, 'An Exalted Naming: The Poetical Fiction of John Banville', *The Canadian Journal of Irish Studies*, vol xiv, no 1, July 1988, 17–27.

McMinn, Joseph, 'Stereotypical Images of Ireland in John Banville's Fiction', *Éire–Ireland*, vol xxiii, no 3, Fall 1988, 94–102.

Molloy, Francis, 'The Search for Truth: The Fiction of John Banville', *Irish University Review*, 29–51.

Outram, Dorinda, 'Heavenly Bodies and Logical Minds', *Graph*, fourth issue, spring 1988, 9–11.

O'Toole, Fintan, 'Stepping into the limelight—and the chaos', *The Irish Times*, 21 October 1989.

Sheenan, Ronan, 'Novelists on the Novel: Interview with John Banville and Francis Stuart', *The Crane Bag*, vol 3, no 1, 1979, 408–16.

Index

Banville, John
  individual works
    Birchwood, 5, 7, 30–45, 53, 55, 65, 74, 81, 87, 99, 101, 105, 107, 109
    The Book of Evidence, 1, 7, 109–23
    Doctor Copernicus, 46–67, 68, 69, 74, 81, 87, 88, 98
    Kepler, 67, 68–87, 88
    Long Lankin, 13–20, 21, 30, 37, 109, 124
    Mefisto, 7, 98–108, 118, 133n.7
    The Newton Letter, 6, 7, 88–97, 98, 111–12
    Nightspawn, 21–9, 30, 31, 45, 65, 99, 107, 108
  allusions, 1–2, 4, 127n.19
  classicism, 5–6
  European tradition, 4, 10
  humanistic ideal, 2, 4, 6
  Irish context and tradition, 6–11
  Modernism, 4, 9–10
  narrators, 5
  novel and dreams, 127n.18
  poetic style, 2
  twins motif, 6, 87, 99–100, 133n.4
Beckett, Samuel, 4, 5, 8, 9, 10, 13, 59
Boccaccio, Giovanni, 28
Booker Prize, 1
Bradbury, Malcolm, 3

Camus, Albert, 109, 113, 134n.4
Carleton, William, 30

Deane, Seamus, 24
Dedalus, Stephen, 8, 43
Descartes, René, 43
Donne, John, 5, 37, 129n.6
Dostoyevsky, Fyodor, 22, 109

Faustian myth, 48, 53, 63, 98, 99, 130n.7, 132n.10

Goethe, Johann, 132n.10, 133n.4
Gide André, 15–16
Grass, Günter, ix
Guinness Peat Aviation Award, 1

Herbert, George, 46
Hofmannsthal, Hugo Von, 88, 95

Imhof, Rüdiger, ix

Joyce, James, 9, 10
  Dubliners, 14, 66
  A Portrait of the Artist as a Young Man, 8–9, 49
  Ulysses, 2, 3, 4, 43

Kearney, Richard, 9
Keats, John, 22, 28, 65, 103, 133n.6
Kiberd, Declan, 127n.17
Koestler, Arthur, 46–7, 54, 58, 71, 77
Kuhn, Thomas, 46–7

Le Fanu, Sheridan, 37
Lernout, Geert, 41, 90
Locke, John, 88
Lodge, David, 3, 129n.8
Lucretius, 19
Lukács, Georg, 2, 4

Magris, Claudio, 98
Mann, Thomas, 5, 130n.7
Marcuse, Herbert, 11–12
Marx, Karl, 21

Nabokov, Vladimir, 5, 30, 37, 129n.7
Newton, Isaac, 1, 88
Nietzsche, Friedrich, 5, 88, 113, 131n.13, 134n.3

O'Brien, Flann, 9

Proust, Marcel, 3, 5, 11, 98
Ptolemy, 51

138 Index

Rilke, Rainer Maria, 5, 68, 82, 96, 132n.9

Shakespeare, William, 37
Shelley, Mary, 109

Somerville and Ross, 30
Stevens, Wallace, 5, 67

Wittgenstein, Ludwig, 44